PUT IT IN THE BOOK!

PUT IT IN THE BOOK!

A Half-Century of Mets Mania

Howie Rose
with Phil Pepe

TRIUMPH
BOOKS

Library of Congress Cataloging-in-Publication Data

Rose, Howie, 1954–
  Put it in the book! : a half-century of Mets mania / Howie Rose with Phil Pepe.
    pages cm
  ISBN 978-1-60078-688-4
  1. New York Mets (Baseball team)—History. 2. New York Mets (Baseball team)—Miscellanea. I. Title.
  GV875.N45R66 2012
  796.357'64097471—dc23
                                2012036988

This book is available in quantity at special discounts for your group or organization. For further information, contact:

Triumph Books
814 North Franklin Street
Chicago, Illinois 60610
(312) 337-0747
www.triumphbooks.com

Printed in U.S.A.
ISBN: 978-1-60078-688-4
Design by Patricia Frey
Photos courtesy of the author unless otherwise indicated

In 1986, a pretty special year as I recall, I met my wife, Barbara. On our second date, she told me that she grew up a Mets fan, and started to reel off the names and uniform numbers of the 1969 world champion Mets. When she came to No. 17 and immediately remembered that it was worn by Rod Gaspar, I was hooked. I guess you could say she had me at Gaspar.

My older daughter Alyssa's first college roommate was actually named Lindsey Nelson (although she spelled her first name differently), but seriously, now. Lindsey Nelson?

My younger daughter Chelsea's first college dormitory was a building called "Shea." I'm not kidding. It could have been named absolutely anything, but it was named Shea.

With material like this, did you think I would wind up working for the Cleveland Indians?

Barbara, Alyssa, and Chelsea are the central figures in my life. If they have been made to feel at any time that my job came before them, I deeply apologize. Family is everything, and I have been blessed with parents, a brother, and a sister who have supported my ambition from its inception. They have my undying love and appreciation.

Barbara, Alyssa, and Chelsea have my heart, my soul, and layers of love that I never knew existed before they came along. This book is dedicated to them.

—Howie Rose, July 2012

CONTENTS

FOREWORD

This was back when I was starting out as a young broadcaster, working for radio station WHN in New York. I spent a lot of time at the station in those days and—this was long before there were cell phones—we would actually pick up a ringing phone in the newsroom.

One day I took a call and it was obvious that the youthful voice on the other end belonged to a teenager who was attempting to sound older than his years. He said his name was Howie Rose and that he called to tell me he'd started a fan club for me. I said I was flattered and offered to help in any way I could.

There were several more phone calls after that, including one in which he asked me—and he was always very polite—if he and a friend could pay a visit to the WHN studios someday to observe what goes on at a real radio station. My first thought was a cynical one—*aha, very clever, that's the reason he started the fan club, so he could get behind the scenes*—but I soon learned that wasn't the case at all; he was serious about the fan club, and he was serious about radio.

I realized early on that not only was Howie a terrific young man, but that he was extremely knowledgeable, had a photographic memory for sports, and, for someone so young, a genuine insight into broadcasting.

In many ways, I saw myself in Howie. When I was young, I was the broadcasting equivalent of a gym rat. Like Howie, I wanted to be around radio and television stations and I formed relationships with two sportscasting icons, Marty Glickman and Les Keiter, who were very supportive, inspiring, and helpful in my career. They both graciously allowed me to visit them and observe a radio station at work.

Because of their kindness to me, I felt a duty to pass along to Howie what had been passed down to me by Glickman and Keiter.

Howie continued to keep in touch. He'd send me copies of a newsletter put out by the fan club, and I'd see him at Rangers games at Madison Square Garden. Howie often would bring a tape recorder to the games, on which he'd practice calling the play-by-play. He'd even send me the tapes and ask me to critique them.

All this time, I was getting flashbacks of the beginning to my own career. Howie was doing all the things I did at his age. What struck me about Howie when I listened to his tapes was how advanced he was in terms of capturing the games. I thought he was exceptional. It's rare to hear someone so young who has all the basics of good sports broadcasting: the knowledge of his subject, the articulation, the smooth delivery, the ability to paint a picture so that the listener knows what's taking place on the field, or the ice. Howie had it all when he was young. I have always enjoyed listening to him and following his progress. He was very good right from the start. He was gifted.

Years later, after I had moved on to NBC television, I had another flashback involving Howie, because he worked at WHN doing reports similar to what I did. To complete the cycle, Howie later became my backup doing Rangers play-by-play on radio and filled in when I was off on other assignments. In fact, in 1994, because of conflicts in my schedule, he ended up doing more games than I did, including the Stanley Cup playoffs when he made the "Matteau! Matteau! Matteau!" call, which was sensational. And in the seventh and final game against Vancouver when the Rangers won the cup, I did two periods and Howie did one.

Then Howie moved on to do Mets games, first on television and then on radio, a dream come true for him having grown up an avid Mets fan. I always thought his work on baseball was excellent. Baseball on radio is a difficult skill because there is so much time to fill between limited action. What I like most about his work is that in addition to being knowledgeable, he is objective. There's no hedging with Howie.

Because of the demands in my own schedule I don't get to hear Howie as much as I'd like during the winter months. I do listen to him more often during the summers, which are not as hectic for me. I've always liked the sound of baseball done well on radio, and Howie is excellent at maintaining that rhythm and pace. I especially like that he treats every game as if he's auditioning for the next one. There's no let-up; it's all good. He's always sharp.

I started out perhaps opening a door or two for Howie, but our relationship has moved on to where now I am his friend and fan. If I were back in my high school days, I would have started a Howie Rose Fan Club.

—Marv Albert

INTRODUCTION

I have this recurring dream: I've only had it for my entire life. I'm in the broadcast booth in a filled-to-capacity Citi Field, Flushing, New York (though when the dream took hold it was at Shea), on a chilly, late-October night, and I'm sitting behind a microphone. In the air there's a buzz of excitement from the huge crowd, there's eager anticipation. Down on the field a baseball game is in progress, the seventh game of the World Series as it happens. Top of the ninth inning with the home team ahead, just one out away from the top of the baseball world, a position they have not occupied in more than a quarter of a century, and I'm poised to deliver great news to a vast radio audience.

Twice in their rather checkered history, the New York Mets have won the World Series. I rejoiced as a fan in the triumph, but alas, I was not directly involved in the euphoria either time.

In 1969, when as the "Miracle Mets" they stunned the baseball world and won their first World Series, I was a 15-year-old high school student, and a fan, clinging to every word uttered by the broadcast team of Lindsey Nelson, Bob Murphy, and Ralph Kiner.

In 1986, when Bill Buckner let Mookie Wilson's easy ground ball get under his glove and two nights later when Jesse Orosco struck out Marty Barrett for the final out, I was working for WCBS radio as a (ahem!) presumably unbiased sports reporter.

My affiliation with the Mets (as host of their pregame show and *Mets Extra* on radio station WFAN and later as play-by-play announcer for Fox Sports New York/MSG and WFAN radio) began in 1987, the year after they won their second World Series. Since then, although they have had some high points, they have not scaled the top of the mountain, and, in fact, have suffered through close calls, disappointments, and underachievement.

I swear the two facts—my affiliation with the Mets and their failure to grab the brass ring—are purely coincidental. *I think!*

I have seen—and in some cases have had to describe—the following:

• Mike Scioscia's two-run home run off Doc Gooden in the top of the ninth of Game 4 of the 1988 National League Championship Series between the Mets and the Los Angeles Dodgers. The Mets, who had won 100 games in the regular season including 10 out of 11 against the Dodgers, led in the series, two games to one, and in the game itself 4–2, but Scioscia's home run off Gooden, an 18-game winner, tied the score. The Dodgers then scored a run in the 12th to win 5–4. Instead of being down three games to one, the Dodgers had tied the Series at two games apiece. Three days later in Los Angeles, Orel Hershiser blanked the Mets 6–0. The Dodgers went to the World Series. The Mets went home.

• The Mets had failed to make the postseason for 10 straight years. They would lose more games than they won for six consecutive seasons, from 1991 to 1996, but the losing ended with the Bobby Valentine era, which began during the 1996 season. In 1999, they won the National League wild-card and beat the Arizona Diamondbacks in four games to advance to the National League Championship Series against the Atlanta Braves.

The Braves won the first three games of the best-of-seven series, but the Mets showed their grit by coming back to win the next two games. In Game 4, they were trailing 2–1 in the bottom of the eighth when John Olerud singled in two runs and the Mets held on for a 3–2 victory. Game 5 was a 15-inning classic with the Mets again battling from behind with two in the bottom of the 15th on Robin Ventura's "grand slam single."

The Braves scored five runs in the first inning of Game 6 and led 5–0 after five. Again the Mets rallied and took the game into extra innings, tied 8–8. The Mets scored a run in the top of the 10th and the Braves tied it in the bottom of that inning. But in the bottom of the 11th the Braves scored on a bases-loaded walk to Andruw Jones, batting against Kenny Rogers, and again the Mets went home without a pennant.

• The Mets were back in the playoffs the following year, winning the wild-card and advancing to the NLCS for the second straight year. This time they beat the St. Louis Cardinals in five games and made it to the World Series for the first time in 14 years. But in that Series the Mets ran into the dynasty that was the Joe Torre–led Yankees and were defeated in five games. The joy of reaching the World Series was definitely diminished by losing to their hated rivals from the Bronx.

We learned in 2000 that the intercity rivalry stimulates the fiscal health of both parties, when the Yankees and Mets combined to draw close to 6 million fans. (Eight years later, in the final season of Shea Stadium and old Yankee Stadium, they would combine to draw more than 8 million fans.)

There was a time (before I was born and until I was four years old) when there were three teams in New York City: the Yankees in the Bronx, the Giants in Manhattan, and the Dodgers in Brooklyn. New York was said to be a National League town, if only by virtue of the two-to-one odds. It was with that belief that the Mets were created, and soon after they arrived they'd grabbed hold of the city and validated the adage of NL supremacy in New York. Once Shea Stadium was erected in 1964, the Mets outdrew the Yankees for 12 consecutive years, from 1964 to 1975, doubling the Yankees' attendance in each of four straight years, from 1969 to 1972.

In the mid-'80s, the Mets enjoyed a resurgence and again surpassed the Yankees in attendance, this time for nine straight seasons, from 1984 to 1992. Then, in 1987, the Mets became the first New York team ever to draw more than 3 million customers with 3,034,129 (the Yankees drew 2,427,672).

Understand as well that attendance figures in those days were computed differently by the two leagues. American League attendance reflected the number of tickets sold, while in the National League only the turnstile count, or "fannies in the seats," counted as paid attendance. Therefore, there were seasons in the mid- and late 1980s, with contending teams on both sides of the rivalry, when the Mets sold roughly half a million more tickets than the Yankees!

History teaches us that success in baseball is cyclical; that neither the good years nor the bad are constant. Believe me, the good ones are a lot more fun, but having the chance to broadcast all of them for the New York Mets has been an honor, a privilege, and a thrill.

If all goes well, the biggest thrill is still to come.

PROLOGUE: NO-NO

The Mets outfielders are standing their ground. Nobody walking around, taking any extra steps between pitches. Santana's 3–1 pitch. Swing and a topper up the third-base line foul. It's 3 and 2.

And now Santana, perhaps a strike away. Johan sweeps a little dirt away from the left of the pitching rubber. Steps behind the rubber. Tugs once at the bill of his cap. Takes a deep breath and steps to the third-base side of the rubber.

Santana into the windup…the payoff pitch on the way…swung on and missed…strike three!

He's done it!

Johan Santana has pitched a no-hitter!

In the eight thousand and twentieth game in the history of the New York Mets, they finally have a no-hitter. And who better to do it than Johan Santana….and what a remarkable story.

His teammates are mobbing him at the mound. The players in the bullpen are trotting in.

It is a surreal feeling here at Citi Field. The first no-hitter in the history of the New York Mets has been pitched by as worthy a candidate as anyone, Johan Santana.

Put it in the books! In the history books!

—My call on WFAN radio of the first no-hitter in Mets history.

It makes no sense that a franchise which has featured Tom Seaver, Nolan Ryan, Dwight Gooden, and David Cone, pitchers that have combined to throw 10 no-hitters for other teams, could go more than 8,000 regular season games since its inception without a no-hitter of its own. But so it was as game time approached at Citi Field on the night of Friday, June 1, 2012.

Game No. 8,020 in Mets' history brought the defending world champion St. Louis Cardinals to town. Before the game, all the commotion was about the return of former Met Carlos Beltran, back in Flushing for the first time since being traded to the Giants the previous July. All anyone seemed focused on leading up to the first inning was what kind of crowd reaction Beltran would get. Johan Santana, the Mets starting pitcher, was almost an afterthought.

In his pregame press conference, Mets' manager Terry Collins insisted that Santana, back after missing a full season recovering from shoulder surgery, would throw no more than 110–115 pitches. When Matt Adams led off the Cardinals' fifth inning with a base on balls, I said on the air that although the Cardinals still did not have a hit, don't expect tonight to be "the night." Santana had already walked four and it appeared he might reach 110 pitches by the seventh inning. But after walking Adams, Santana retired the next nine hitters and started the eighth inning with an 8–0 lead, just six outs away from Mets history. The fact that in the sixth inning there was a blown call by third-base umpire Adrian Johnson on Beltran's line drive down the third-base line didn't matter. Replays would show that Beltran's drive actually kicked up chalk from the foul line beyond third base and should have been ruled a fair ball; but it wasn't, and the no-hitter, if not Terry Collins' stomach, was intact.

Collins agonized visibly over his decision, but against his better judgment and his own pregame directive to keep Santana's pitch count under control, he allowed Johan to continue his bid for a no-hitter despite a high pitch count. Santana walked his fifth batter with two out in the eighth, but at this point Terry was uncomfortably committed to

Johan Santana waves to the Citi Field crowd after finishing the first no-hitter in Mets history on June 1, 2012. (AP Images)

his pitcher's pursuit of history. Collins wasn't the only one compromising his principles. I had always been blunt on the air by using the words "no-hitter" in describing what a pitcher was pursuing. Most broadcasters subscribe to baseball superstition by talking around a no-hitter in progress, but I figured I didn't control what happened on the field so I decided to simply report the facts and let the game take care of itself.

I don't know why I decided to make this night different, but I did. I found *myself* compromising *my* principles by saying such things as, "It's 8–0 New York and the Mets have all the hits and all the runs." I left no doubt what Santana was attempting to accomplish, but I never uttered the phrase "no-hitter," and I admit doing so caused me to feel slightly squirrelly. By the ninth inning, all I felt was intense, nervous anxiety.

I had never broadcast a no-hitter, never had so much as seen one in person. But as the final inning began I had a feeling that no matter how badly I wanted it, no matter how badly the fans and anyone connected to the Mets wanted it, there was some external force at work which decreed that no New York Met would pitch a no-hitter. Not now. Not ever.

Tom Seaver had taken three no-hitters into the ninth inning as a Met only to allow hits to such luminaries as Jimmy Qualls, Leron Lee, and Joe Wallis. Kit Pellow and Paul Hoover also had broken up Mets' no-hit bids in the eighth inning. Don't bother looking for plaques of those five spoilers in Cooperstown. You won't find them.

By the ninth inning, I had a knot in my stomach, the same sort of knot I had experienced calling those dramatic Rangers games during their run to the 1994 Stanley Cup. I was trapped at the corner of Professional and Emotional, a dangerous intersection. When Matt Holliday, leading off the ninth, got out in front of a changeup and looped a pop-fly to shallow center, my voice reflected uncertainty that the ball would drop for a hit. It didn't. It hung up long enough for Andres Torres to make the catch. One out! The next batter, Allen Craig, then hit one a little harder to left field, but Kirk Nieuwenhuis made a running catch. Two outs!

The next hitter was David Freese, the 2011 World Series MVP. Santana fell behind in the count 3–0 and was now at 131 pitches, more than he had ever thrown in a single game in his career. A walk to Freese would bring to the plate Yadier Molina of all people, whose home run in Game 7 of the 2006 National League Championship Series had broken the spirit of the Mets. Imagine Santana's no-hit bid coming down to an at-bat by one of the Mets all-time heartbreakers.

Santana found the strike zone with his next two pitches to Freese, filling the count at 3–2. He was one strike away from history. He went into his windup and fired. Freese took a mighty swing at a vintage Santana changeup…and missed. I was in a state of broadcasting shock, a feeling I had never before experienced. The Citi Field crowd of 27,069 must have felt the same way. Johan Santana and the Mets had finally achieved a no-hitter.

I'm comfortable in the thought that my call of that final pitch, that moment in Mets history, reflected the enormity of the achievement while still paying attention to detail. It took me almost 60 seconds after the final pitch to say, "Put it in the books! In the history books!"

I'm proud of that because there was so much else to describe that seemed of greater importance at that moment than being able to squeeze in a signature call immediately upon history having been made. I was a little hysterical at times, but it is one of my favorite calls.

Later, Gary Cohen came from the TV side to the radio booth and joined me for a special postgame show. Two New York kids who grew up with the Mets, suffering their failures and exulting in their successes, reminiscing and glowing over the ultimate success, attaining the seemingly unattainable, a no-hitter. It was a momentous night in Mets history and one of the most memorable nights of my career.

After the postgame show, I went to the Mets clubhouse hoping to offer Santana private congratulations. Thankfully, he was still there 90 minutes after the game had ended. I gave him a congratulatory hug and told him I had never cried on the air, but this night I came close to breaking up a bit.

"Did you cry?" he asked with a smile.

When I said I didn't, he seemed so disappointed I wished that I'd told him a little white lie. Then I did something I had never done before in almost four decades of sports broadcasting. I asked Johan to sign the scorecard of the game I had just broadcast.

That's how much that game and that night meant to Johan Santana, to the entire Mets organization, to their fans and, I confess, to me.

Chapter 1
I Confess

In the interest of full disclosure, I have a confession to make: my father was a Yankees fan (so was I, but only when I was a little guy and only before there was a team called the New York Mets).

The first baseball game I can remember is the seventh game of the 1960 World Series between the Yankees and the Pittsburgh Pirates. When I was little, my dad would grill me on the Yankees' lineup, so I knew their names, their numbers, and their positions. For instance, I knew the name Yogi Berra. I knew he was No. 8 and that he was a catcher. The vague recollection I have of Game 7 of the '60 World Series is of Bill Mazeroski hitting the game-winning home run over the head of the Yankees' left fielder, Berra. My six-year-old mind could not grasp the concept of someone taking off all of that catcher's equipment and running all the way out to left field and still almost catching Mazeroski's home run. (It's a minor miracle I actually became a big-league broadcaster.)

Because of my dad and his love of the Yankees, I became immersed in baseball in 1961, a magical season in which Roger Maris and Mickey Mantle chased Babe Ruth's supposedly unbreakable single-season home run record of 60 and doing it before my father's and my eyes, practically in our backyard, in fact.

At the time we lived in the Bronx, only a few blocks from Yankee Stadium. I was born in Brooklyn (can't everybody trace at least part of his roots to Brooklyn?) but when I was five we moved to the Bronx, where I attended P.S. 77 for first and second grades. I mention that only because P.S. 77 was across the street from James Monroe High School, where both Hall of Famer Hank Greenberg and the Mets' Ed Kranepool went to high school. Literally, when I was sitting in my classroom in P.S. 77, Kranepool was hitting home runs for James Monroe toward my classroom. That shows how far back my New York Mets roots go.

Not surprising, kids being notorious front-runners, my first baseball hero was Maris (the Mets, Tom Seaver, Bud Harrelson, Darryl Strawberry, Keith Hernandez, Mookie Wilson, Gary Carter, and David Wright were not yet even on my radar). I have vivid recollections of the final week of that season with Maris closing in on the record. I'd watch the games on television, but I was in second grade and if there was a night game and there was school the next day, I had to go to bed. I couldn't stay up until 10:00 or 10:30 PM to watch the game. My dad and I would catch the start of a game together in my bedroom. He'd keep the TV on, but he'd turn the sound down and he'd allow me to stay up a little later. When he thought it was too late for me to stay awake any longer, he'd make me turn around and go to sleep while he watched the rest of the game. It wasn't an easy chore for him to get me to sleep because I kept cheating and stealing peeks at the television.

On September 20, a Wednesday night, the Yankees were playing the Orioles in Baltimore. I watched the beginning of the game and then I dropped off to sleep. I was asleep when Maris hit his 59th home run, and my dad was so excited he literally shook me awake to show me Maris running around the bases. That's how passionate he was about baseball and the Yankees.

The following year the Mets were born and I dropped my allegiance to the Yankees and became a Mets fan for the same reason so many kids of my age did at the time: the Mets were not our father's team, they were ours. It was a chance to get in on the action from day one. I was narcissistic enough to believe that because I had become such a huge

Here I am in my second-grade class photo (third row, far left), standing next to my teacher, Mrs. Hoberman. She and Jacqueline Kennedy were my first crushes!

baseball fan in '61, that when this new team showed up the next year, it was created just for me: "Here's your gift! You're a baseball fan? Here's a team of your own."

That's why I adopted the Mets; they were my team, a team created just for me. I'm sure I wasn't the only eight-year-old who believed that.

I don't imagine there are too many people who can say they have been fans of a certain team since day one of that team's existence. Happily, I am one of those few.

Throughout spring training of 1962, I absolutely peppered my father with questions about the players who would make up the original New York Mets. I needed to know everything about everyone. Obviously, he knew players with New York roots such as Gil Hodges, Charlie Neal, and Roger Craig. He was quite familiar with National League veterans like Richie Ashburn and Frank Thomas. Somehow, though, he didn't have a great deal of material on Rod Kanehl and Jim Hickman, but thanks to original announcers Lindsey Nelson, Bob Murphy, and Ralph Kiner, there were plenty of games to watch and listen to in the spring. I should only have studied for tests in school as diligently as I pursued information about New York's new National League ballclub.

The Topps chewing gum company was a big help, too. They, of course, were the producers of baseball cards (the 1962 set was always my favorite, with the faux wood paneling design on the front of the cards), and the information printed on the back gave you at least a glimpse into what kind of a player was depicted on the front. Even then, knowledge was power.

The first game the Mets ever played was on Wednesday night, April 11, against the Cardinals in St. Louis. I couldn't stay up to watch the entire game, but I remember getting ready for school the next morning and going into my parents' room before my dad left for work and saying, "How did the Mets do?"

"They lost," my dad said, two words that I would hear all too often over the next few years. Immediately, I felt bad. I guess I was hooked.

History will record that the final score of the first game the Mets ever played was 11–4 with Larry Jackson beating Roger Craig. Julian Javier had four hits for the Cards, Bill White knocked in three runs, and the great Stan "the Man" Musial was 3-for-3 with two RBI. Gus Bell got the first hit in Mets' history, a single in the second inning. Charlie Neal knocked in the Mets' first run, and Gil Hodges, fittingly, hit the first home run in franchise history.

With my beautiful wife, Barbara, cruising around Manhattan.
(Photo: Marc. S. Levine, New York Mets)

I was disappointed with the result, but from that point, at age eight, I was off and running. From that day on, I became immersed in the Mets, obsessed with them.

I remember the first home game in Mets' history, on April 13 (Friday the 13th, wouldn't you know?) against the Pirates at the old Polo Grounds. Only 12,447 showed up for that historic occasion on a cold, raw, drizzly day to see the Mets lose again, 4–3 this time, with Tom Sturdivant outpitching Sherman "Road Block" Jones.

And I remember the first win in Mets' history. They would lose their first nine games before finally winning one in Pittsburgh on April 23, a 9–1 blowout of the Pirates behind Jay Hook's complete-game five-hitter. Unfortunately, the Mets would win only 39 more games that season, while losing 120.

I went to only one game at the Polo Grounds in that first year and it turned out to be a historic one: Friday night, July 6, 1962. It was the night Gil Hodges hit his 370th and last major league home run, passing Ralph Kiner on the all-time list for the most home runs by a right-handed batter in National League history. It came in the second inning against Ray Sadecki. The Mets beat the Cardinals 10–3, so you can imagine what a happy young guy I was.

Later that summer we moved from the Bronx to Bayside, for me another fortuitous event, another sign that I was destined to be a Mets fan. Two years later, the Mets moved into their brand-new home, Shea Stadium, leaving the Polo Grounds in Manhattan and taking up residence in Flushing, only a short distance from my new home. Now there was no doubt in my mind that this was all done to accommodate me. I was able to feed my passion for the Mets with frequent trips to Shea Stadium, which would have been much more difficult if we were still living in the Bronx.

The first game I went to without adult supervision was Opening Day on April 15, 1966. The Mets played the Atlanta Braves, and with Shea Stadium still practically brand new, a crowd of better than 52,000 showed up to watch Jack Fisher oppose the Braves' Denny Lemaster.

The Mets jumped in front in the bottom of the first when Ron Hunt walked, stole second, went to third on catcher Joe Torre's throw into center field, and scored on Ken Boyer's sacrifice fly. The Braves tied it with a run in the sixth, knocked in on a single by Hank Aaron. The Mets grabbed the lead in the eighth on Cleon Jones' home run, but in the top of the ninth, the Braves tied the score on a single and took the lead with a squeeze bunt. The Mets went down in the bottom of the ninth and were beaten 3–2.

It was a heartbreaking defeat, especially discouraging for a 12-year-old kid who had high hopes for his favorite team. But it was something I was going to have to get used to if I intended to continue following my team, which I did.

Once I was able to go to games without an adult, my friends and I started going regularly, maybe to 20 or 30 games a season. We found we could take the Q27 bus from Springfield Boulevard and 73rd Avenue in Bayside to Main Street in downtown Flushing, and from there we could either take the subway one stop to Shea Stadium or walk across the Roosevelt Avenue Bridge. Invariably, we opted for walking across the bridge in order to save the subway fare, which then became a hot dog, an ice cream, or a scorecard. The trip from portal to portal was less than an hour.

We used to get the same seats in the upper deck, where all seats, except for the first few rows, were general admission and cost $1.30. The gates opened for a 2:00 PM game at noon and we'd buy our tickets and then run up the ramp or onto the escalator and settle into the same seats: Section 1, right behind home plate, Row 1, the first row behind the reserved section. This may have been an omen as well, because our broadcast booth at Shea was right behind home plate, just below where my seats had been. We carved our initials into those seats, as if to mark them as reserved. If those seats had not been replaced by plastic ones in 1980 when Shea received a makeover, I would have loved to have bought them as a memento. I trust they would have cost more than $1.30!

In the future I'd be able to actually interview Mets greats like Cleon Jones, here at an oldtimer's game in the 1980s. (Photo: Peter Simon)

There was a game in 1966 that still resonates, so much so that I committed the date to memory. It was August 4, a Thursday afternoon, the Mets against the Giants in Shea Stadium. As was customary in those early days, whenever the recently departed Dodgers or Giants came to town there was always a packed house at Shea. On this day, more than 41,000 were in attendance, many of them no doubt drawn by the opportunity to see Willie Mays one more time.

The Mets were facing Juan Marichal, whom they had never beaten. At the time he was 15–0 against them, No. 15 having come just two nights earlier when manager Herman Franks brought him into the game in the eighth inning and he pitched a perfect inning and a third and got the win, improving his record that season to 17–4. Now, some 40 hours later, he was starting and shooting for win No. 18 on the season.

Marichal had picked right up where he left off two nights earlier by retiring the first 15 Mets and taking his perfect game into the bottom of the sixth, leading 3–0. When the first two Mets batters were retired in the sixth, Mets manager Wes Westrum let pitcher Dennis Ribant hit, and he broke up Marichal's perfect game by dribbling a 38-hopper over the pitcher's mound into center field. (We could never figure out Westrum.)

Marichal started the ninth and gave up a home run to make it 6–5 before leaving the game. The rally continued and the Mets won it on a three-run pinch-hit home run by Ron Swoboda off Bill Henry. I was so excited leaving the ballpark that day that I kept thinking, "This is the greatest game I ever saw [I was only 12], and the greatest game I ever will see. I'm going to remember this day forever. August 4, 1966."

I also remember on my way home thinking, "I wonder what it must have been like to call that home run. How excited were Lindsey Nelson and Bob Murphy calling the home run on television and radio? What did they say? How did they phrase it? Did they know right away that it was a home run?"

They didn't have the benefit of replays back then, so it was a lingering curiosity that I maintained forever. Most kids, when they went to a game and saw someone hit a game-winning home run, would imagine themselves being the guy that hit the home run. Not me. I would fantasize about being the guy that called the home run on radio or television. How had the announcers made it sound? How would I have made it sound?

I knew I was never going to be the guy that hit the game-winning home run in the bottom of the ninth, so I figured the next best thing was to be the guy that described that home run.

My dad didn't treat me as a turncoat because I abandoned his Yankees and embraced the Mets as my team. Nonetheless he seemed to take great joy in teasing me about following such a woeful collection of losers in those early days when his Yankees were winning championship after championship while my Mets were setting records for futility. He made fun of me for being a Mets fan.

That all changed in 1969, though, and I think he got almost as big a kick out of the Mets miracle run to win the World Series as I did. Sadly, he didn't live long enough to see me become a broadcaster for the Mets. He would have liked that, and I'm certain I would have succeeded in getting him to switch his allegiance from his team to mine.

Like most city kids, I tried my hand at playing all sports—Little League baseball, softball, stickball, stoop ball, touch football, basketball in the playground, roller hockey—changing the sport with the changing of the seasons, hoping, or more likely fantasizing, that some professional scout would recognize my latent talent and sign me to a contract. It never happened. I never was even good enough to make the varsity at my high school in any sport, so I contented myself with being the super fan and nurturing my dream of becoming a sportscaster.

I can't pinpoint when I first had that thought but I know it was early. Maybe it was the first time I heard Mel Allen say, "Going… going…gone!" I was enthralled by the whole idea of being in the broadcast booth and making a living out of going to a baseball game. From the first baseball game I attended I was smitten with the whole environment. Like most other kids I said I wanted to be a baseball player when I grew up, but during Little League I realized that wasn't going to happen.

So I switched gears and fantasized about how it would feel to call the big moment, not to be in the moment as a player, but to call it.

As a kid, I was totally immersed in sports, obsessed with them; hockey in the winter, baseball in the spring and summer. Nothing else in my life mattered. Nothing! So when my parents told me I had to go to Hebrew school for bar mitzvah training I argued with my mom and dad like you wouldn't believe. Billy Martin and Earl Weaver, in their best days arguing with the umps, had nothing on me.

"You mean to tell me you want me to go to school until three o'clock, come home, drop my books off, and then go to school again and miss the entire Mets game? Are you nuts?"

As a sort of compromise, I went to a Hebrew school that was unique. It was expensive to send kids to a conventional Hebrew school with a structured environment. It was my good fortune to grow up as a Baby Boomer in an environment where most families had two or three kids, and so my parents simply could not afford the tuition needed to send their three kids to a conventional Hebrew school.

In our neighborhood, there was a man named Joel Bernstein who said he was a rabbi and he had a plan. His niece lived in a two-family house and they converted the basement of the house into a school by putting a divider in the middle of the room to create two classrooms. He charged minimal, affordable tuition for kids to come for Hebrew school training. We learned to read in Hebrew—just enough to qualify for our bar mitzvah—but we didn't learn much else.

Rabbi Bernstein also had a connection on Manhattan's lower east side, where he would buy tape recorders, walkie-talkies, and transistor radios, and make Hebrew school into a competition. He broke the class up into quadrants, four students to a quadrant, and we went around the room reading from the Hebrew book. Whichever team made the fewest mistakes during the reading would get so many points, and whatever team had the most points after a set period won tape recorders, walkie-talkies, or transistor radios. We were being bribed into learning Hebrew.

Part of our curriculum included reading from a periodical called *Jewish Current Events*. On the back of the periodical was a list of 10 questions. Hebrew school kids were going to be rowdy by nature simply because there wasn't the supervision in Hebrew school that there was in regular school. We'd occasionally take liberties, and when Rabbi Bernstein had had enough of our hijinks he'd get angry and say, "Okay, we're not playing today. We're not competing today. We're going to take the test. Get out your copy of *Jewish Current Events*. There are 10 questions on the back, answer the questions."

Nobody took the test seriously. What was Bernstein going to do to us if we failed? Throw us out of his school? We didn't think so.

All these years later, I still remember one of the questions: What position does Moishe Dayan play in Israel's defense?

I wrote: Shortstop.

And the guy that gave that answer, almost a half-century later, on April 29, 2012, was inducted into The National Jewish Sports Hall of Fame and Museum.

Chapter 2
MIRACLE

In August 2009, it was my privilege to serve as the on-field host at Citi Field for a ceremony commemorating the 40th anniversary of the Mets miracle run to the National League pennant and the world championship. Did I say privilege? It was more than that. Considering the circumstances and my long history as a Mets fan, it was a thrill beyond compare.

The simple fact is that, for me, nothing ever will beat the excitement of the 1969 season, because at the time I was 15 years old—the perfect age to be a fan—and very impressionable. And now here I was, 40 years later, having just introduced members of that '69 team, standing on the outfield grass in short-center field as the national anthem played prior to the start of a regular season game between the Mets and Philadelphia Phillies.

I looked up at the flag waving in the summer breeze and couldn't help thinking, "This is great! What a kick this is. It's like being a player for 30 seconds."

I glanced to my left and there was Nolan Ryan and Bud Harrelson. I glanced to my right and there was Tom Seaver and Jerry Koosman. I was having an out-of-body experience. For a few fleeting seconds I got flushed in this dream sequence. Here I am standing at attention and there's Seaver and Koosman, Ryan and Harrelson. What am I doing here? What sense does this make? It was quite a profound feeling.

All these years later I can still remember back to '69. Before the start of the season nobody—and I mean *nobody*—was predicting the Mets would accomplish very much. In their first seven years, the Mets had finished in 10th place five times and in ninth twice. The most wins they'd had in any season had been 73 the previous year. To think they would even win as many games as they lost in '69 was far-fetched. But their 73 wins under new manager Gil Hodges in '68 did represent a 12-game improvement over the previous year, and that was enough for my friends and me to be somewhat encouraged by the pitching posse they were putting together. I was hopeful going into the '69 season but still unfulfilled. I remember I told my friends, "I'm really getting tired of losing. I'm getting impatient."

When I was a teenager, summers meant wall-to-wall, dawn-to-dusk baseball. Following my beloved Mets and playing on a couple of summer league teams, one of them coached by a man named Bob Arnone, who, we were told, had played minor league ball in the Pittsburgh Pirates farm system and was a stickler for fundamentals. This one day after a game Coach Arnone took the entire team to the sliding pits to teach us the correct way to slide. Sliding pits? For a sandlot team? This guy was serious. Generally, I loved it.

Coach Arnone had us go back and forth—hands up, head back—the whole thing. As the session dragged on, I was getting antsy. My lifelong friend Robert Joseph and I had tickets to the Mets game against the Cubs that night and we were nervous that we might miss the start of the game or arrive too late to occupy our favorite seats behind home plate. Unforgivable sins for the Mets' two greatest fans. We were more concerned with the fortunes of the Mets than we were of our own team. What difference did it make if we didn't know the proper way to slide as long as Bud Harrelson and Tommie Agee did?

We kept telling Coach Arnone, "We've got to get going. We've got tickets to the Mets game tonight."

"You'll go to the Mets game when you get this right."

We never bought tickets in advance back then because with 55,000 seats in Shea Stadium and the entire upper deck available for general

One of my biggest thrills, emceeing the 40ᵗʰ anniversary celebration and reunion of the 1969 Mets at Citi Field. (Photo: Marc S. Levine, New York Mets)

admission, we were never shut out. We didn't have tickets this night, either. We figured we'd get to the stadium early, as usual, purchase our tickets and be in the front of the line when the gates opened, then we'd run up and get our customary seats in Section 1, behind home plate. But Coach Arnone was messing with our plans.

To put my anxiety in perspective, the date was July 9, 1969, a famous and important one in Mets history. The afternoon before, the Mets had come from behind with three runs in the bottom of the ninth off Ferguson Jenkins and beat the Cubs 4–3 on Ed Kranepool's game-winning RBI single. They'd cut the Cubs lead to 4½ games and now they had their young ace, Tom Seaver, ready to go with a chance to cut the lead to 3½ games.

When Coach Arnone figured we had mastered the sliding technique enough to equal Ty Cobb as terrors on the basepaths, he dismissed us. It was 4:40 PM and we were running late. We dashed home, showered quickly, changed clothes, and at 6:30 began our trek to Shea Stadium that normally took us about an hour. The game was scheduled to start at 8:00, so we still had an hour and a half to get to Shea, buy our tickets, and dash upstairs to our regular seats. We knew the stadium was going to be packed and we were too late to be there when the gates opened, but we weren't worried.

We were waiting for the bus that took us from Bayside to Flushing when along came our friend Barry Berman riding his bicycle.

"Where are you guys going?" he said.

"We're going to the Mets game."

"Oh, you got tickets?"

"Nah, we'll get 'em there."

He said, "Are you nuts? There's no way you're going to get in. The place is going to be packed. It's gonna be a sellout. There's no chance you're getting tickets."

"Not only are we getting in," Robert said knowingly, "but Seaver's going to pitch a perfect game and you're not going to be there."

"I'll bet you a million dollars he doesn't pitch a perfect game."

"You're on," Robert said.

We managed to get to Shea Stadium in time to get tickets and were even able to get our usual seats and, of course, that was the night Seaver pitched 8⅓ perfect innings, and then, two outs away from a perfect game, gave up the hit to Jimmy Qualls. Seaver got the last two outs and the Mets beat the Cubs 4–0 to climb to within three games of first place.

Even more than the one-hit shutout, what I remember most about that game was Seaver coming to bat in the bottom of the eighth inning, leading 4–0, with 11 strikeouts, three outs away from perfection and so dominant that the only question was whether he was going to pitch the first no-hitter in Mets' history.

Al Weis had singled in front of him and up came Seaver. The ovation started as soon as he came out of the dugout and went to the on-deck circle. It continued while he got into the batter's box and it was still going when Seaver bunted the first pitch and did something that I bet even Tom would say was one of the most mindless or embarrassing things he's ever done on a baseball field. After laying down the bunt, instead of running to first base as he was supposed to, he peeled off, made a right turn, and headed back to the dugout, later explaining that he was so zoned into his perfect game that he never realized what he did. All the while, the thunderous ovation never stopped. It lasted from the moment he appeared in the on-deck circle until he was back in the dugout after his bunt, probably 40 seconds to a minute of nonstop cheering and applause.

I distinctly remember thinking to myself, "We have our Mantle, our DiMaggio, our Koufax. We've arrived." At the time the Mets were eight years old, but July 9, 1969, was the night they were bar mitzvahed.

Many years later, I had the opportunity to tell Seaver about the bet I had with my friend Barry Berman and kidded Tom that he cost me half a million dollars. (P.S. I never did find out if Barry Berman had a million bucks.)

Interesting sidenote: In 1994, on July 9, the 25th anniversary of Seaver's gem, I did a live radio interview with Jimmy Qualls, who was on the phone from his home. I asked Qualls if he and Seaver had ever discussed that night, and Qualls' hit, and Jimmy's reply was a classic. He said that the following week when the Mets played the Cubs in Chicago, Seaver came up to him during batting practice and said, "You little [so and so], you cost me a million bucks!" For the record, Seaver denies having ever talked to Qualls on that or any other day, but it made me wonder, considering Tom's hypothetical windfall, as well as mine, if Barry Berman and Tom Seaver actually knew each other!

I firmly believe that Seaver's near-perfect game and the 4–0 victory was the turning point for the Mets—the night it all came together. From that night on, the Mets were no longer the joke of the National League.

That was the most memorable night I have ever spent at Shea Stadium. I've seen them win the National League East division there, the National League pennant, even the World Series, but that night, July 9, 1969, was the seminal moment in my life as a baseball fan. I left the ballpark and went home thinking that the Mets were for real and they might even be good enough to do the impossible.

The '69 Mets clinched first place on September 24, a Wednesday night, when Gary Gentry beat the Cardinals and Steve Carlton 6–0 on a complete-game four-hitter. Donn Clendenon hit two home runs and I was there with two of my friends, Robert Joseph and Eric Friedenthal, and 54,925 other people.

During the bottom of the eighth, my friends and I had a brainstorm. Let's run downstairs and wait in the aisle of the field boxes and as soon as the final out of the game is made, we'll run onto the field. We were three idiots that thought this was a great idea, that nobody else would think of such a thing and we'd be the only ones on the field.

Wrong!

Here's what happened. We were sitting in the upper deck and after the third out in the bottom of the eighth we sprinted down the ramp to the field level. We went inside the vestibule where normally you could see the field, only this time we couldn't see a thing. Every aisle was packed with fans waiting to do exactly what we were planning to do. How dare they rain on our parade?

Without a word, we turned tail and went back up the ramp to the loge level and stood behind home plate, the three of us with a single thought: after all these years of going to Mets games at Shea Stadium—it was only five years, but it felt like forever—there was no way we were going to miss that last pitch and the clinching of the division. This is what we lived for.

We watched the final pitch from right below the TV cameras. I had with me a small, blue shopping bag, inside of which was a bunch of ripped-up newspapers, my makeshift version of confetti, and when Joe Torre grounded into a double play—shortstop Bud Harrelson to second baseman Al Weis to first baseman Donn Clendenon—to end the game, and the Mets were officially champions of the National League East, I unloaded my "confetti" into the air. That's my contribution to Mets history. If you watch the film of that clinching you can see confetti floating in the air. I guarantee that's my homemade confetti on that film because I was right where the TV cameras were. After unloading the confetti, my friends and I ran out onto the field, joined there by 20,000 other delirious Mets fans.

The clincher happened to come on "Fan Appreciation Night" and all fans got a Mets key chain that came in a little plastic wrap that could be closed. So I tore up some Shea Stadium turf, stuffed it in with the key chain, and brought it home where it would sit on a shelf in my bedroom for years.

My mother asked, "What did you bring home?"

"Center field, Mom." She was never quite convinced, thinking it was a different kind of grass.

The '69 season was the first year of the League Championship Series, and now the Mets were going to put playoff tickets on sale and I was determined to be there, by hook or by crook.

It was a best-of-five series, with the first two games to be played in Atlanta and Game 3 and, if necessary, Games 4 and 5, back in Shea. I had no money to go to three playoff games. It was all I could do just to scrounge up enough money from my parents to go to one game. So my friends and I decided we'd try to get tickets for Game 3, which was the only one scheduled at Shea that was certain to be played. We arranged for Robert Joseph's father to drop us off at Shea Stadium on his way to work at about 4:30 AM on the day tickets went on sale. We waited for the ticket booths to open and were able to buy tickets.

Game 3 at Shea was going to be played on Monday afternoon, October 6, which presented a small problem for me. I was attending Benjamin N. Cardozo High School, which was so crowded that students were split into two sessions. I was on the late session with classes from 12:30 in the afternoon to 6:00 at night. Nothing was going to stop me from going to that game, but in order to do so I told my parents I was going to have to miss school that day. Knowing how much it meant to me, they said it was okay with them.

As luck would have it, my parents, who never went anywhere—I never remember them even taking a vacation—were committed to go to Brown's Hotel in the Catskills for a seminar that weekend. They had planned to leave on Friday morning and, because I was on late session, they told me I could miss school on Friday. I was delighted with that information and reminded my parents that I was also going to miss school on Monday to attend the Mets playoff game. I don't remember them giving me any flak about that. So here I was, looking forward to an extended weekend vacation, a couple of days in the Catskills, ending with the Mets playoff game on Monday.

The Mets won the two games in Atlanta, crushing the Braves 9–5 and 11–6, so my friends and I congratulated ourselves for making the right choice in getting tickets for Game 3. As a bonus, we got to see the Mets clinch the pennant with a 7–4 win.

The euphoria was such that we didn't want the day to end, so to prolong it my friends and I took up a vigil outside the Diamond Club entrance, where we knew the players entered and exited the stadium, hoping to catch a glimpse of one of our conquering heroes. We agreed that we would wait until the last player left, and we were so delirious with joy we didn't care if that meant waiting until midnight.

We'd waited more than an hour when we figured it was time to leave, so we started walking toward the train station. As we did, we noticed a car parked at the curb near the station. The window on the driver's side was rolled down and we peeked into the car and saw Jerry Grote, the Mets' catcher, sitting all by himself, probably waiting for a teammate.

Grote had the reputation of being a hothead, on and off the field. He didn't like signing autographs and he had a tendency to be ornery and irascible, but he was a favorite of mine. I'd often read that Grote was difficult and uncooperative with the writers; but what did I care how he was with the writers? He was throwing out Lou Brock all the time. As a fan that's all I cared about. Besides he had just helped his team clinch the National League East, so we figured if ever there was a time to get him in even a semblance of a good mood, this was it.

My friends and I looked at each other as if to summon up the courage to approach this ogre. We made a pact. "Let's be cool," we said. "Let's ask him nicely and make certain not to bump into his car."

We sheepishly sidled up to the car and asked him for his autograph. To our delight and surprise he didn't chase us away.

"All right," he said, "I'll sign for you, but don't tell anybody I'm here." I'm not sure, but I think we kept his secret.

I came home from the pennant-clinching game in a state of euphoria. Forget the little plastic bag of turf I brought home from the division clincher, this time I came home wearing half of center field. I burst through the door, shouting, "We did it; we won the pennant!" My dad glared at me and said, as only an irate father can, "Where were you?"

I tried to explain that I was at the Mets game and that I had told them I was going to miss school on Monday, but my father was not hearing any of it. He was irate because our home had been visited by the truant officer, making me the first kid since Spanky and Alfalfa to get a visit from said truant officer, who was suspicious because I had been absent on Friday and the following Monday.

My parents were so incensed and/or embarrassed by that visit from the truant officer that they chose to punish me by not giving me money for tickets to the World Series.

I was devastated. Here was my team playing in the World Series in only the eighth year of their existence, and I, their loyal fan, after suffering through so much disappointment, heartbreak, and defeat, was not going to see any of the games. But while I couldn't get to Shea Stadium, I was determined not to miss a single pitch, either on the radio or on television.

Geometry never was going to be my strength in high school. I had a better chance of pitching Game 1 of the '69 World Series than I did figuring out the hypotenuse of a triangle or proving required theorem

Fans fill the field at Shea Stadium on Monday, October 6, 1969, after the Mets won the National League pennant. I'm the one with the big smile, waving my index finger and yelling, "We're number one." (AP Images)

No. 12, but the Mets' success provided enough of a distraction that I was forced to play catch-up all year, beginning on October 17.

Once the World Series was over and the Mets were world champions, I realized how much geometry had slipped away during my preoccupation with baseball. I found myself much further behind than even the Mets had been in mid-August. I was geometrically gone, literally failing every test that I took in Mr. Banner's class. I couldn't pass a geometry test if my life depended on it.

Suddenly it was June 1970 and I was in huge trouble. Mr. Banner told me that I was a nice kid, always showed up, caused no trouble and posted no bills, but he was going to give me an ultimatum. "I'd love to pass you," he said, "so I'll give you a choice. You can either pass the class final or the regents. You don't have to pass both tests. If you pass either one of them, you will pass the course."

Well, I failed the class final and now I was down to an 0–2 count and Nolan Ryan was throwing his 100 mph fastball. It was either pass the Regents or I would get a failing grade for the term, and then I'd have to make the course up the following year or in summer school. You tell a 16-year-old kid he has to go to summer school, especially a kid so obsessed with baseball, and you might as well take him out and shoot him. Vegas immediately installed me a 200-to-1 underdog. This is where the Mets came in.

After my parents hired a tutor to help try to pull off the impossible—a palpable waste of money—I took practice Regents after practice Regents, and the early results were not good. However, at the depths of my discouragement, I channeled the Mets. I know this sounds corny and perhaps a bit contrived, but I implore you to trust me on this. However frustrated I became, I reminded myself over and over how the Mets pulled it off and won the World Series. I kept telling myself the Mets did it, I'm going to do it; that just like the Mets, if I believed I could pass the Regents and I kept working hard, then somehow I would.

Each night, as Regents day approached, I went to sleep replaying those great moments from the previous fall in my mind. They inspired me to work harder than I had ever worked on anything in school before or after the great geometry crossroads. Gradually, things began to make sense, and when I showed up to take that test I wasn't in my seat alone. Gil Hodges, his coaching staff, and those 25 special players were with me, and believe it or not, with no crib notes, cheating, or any such shenanigans, I pulled off a test score of 87! All I needed to pass the course was a final grade of 65, but Mr. Banner was so thrilled he gave me a 75, which I really didn't deserve.

I turned that geometry textbook into the '69 Baltimore Orioles. I'm not sure that my entire year's worth of test scores before the Regents ever even added up to 87, but to this day I remain fully convinced that there is no way I would have passed that test without the inspiration and motivation provided by the '69 Mets.

I'm sure mine is not the only such story, and that remains the everlasting legacy of the '69 Mets. They're not a team so much as they are an entity, a force, an example of self-confidence and hard work producing desired results. Great pitching didn't hurt, either.

As a parent, I have tried to hand that message down to my children, to teach them that nothing is beyond their reach if they're willing to work hard for it and to believe in themselves and, hopefully, some day they can impart that thinking to their children. That's the '69 Mets, the gift that keeps on giving.

I think back to how perfect that '69 season was, the poetically brilliant choreography of Cleon Jones going down on one knee to punctuate the final out of the World Series. I think, too, of my English teacher at Cardozo High, one Paul Freda, and how he allowed us to listen to the end of that final game in his class with one stipulation, that as soon as it ended, we were to turn off the radios and get back to reading the epic poem *The Rime of the Ancient Mariner* by Samuel Taylor Coleridge.

That poem is a literary classic, but to a 15-year-old, delirious over the Mets just having won the World Series, it was an unfortunate segue. However, a deal was a deal, and even with the class half-crazy with delight, Mr. Freda began to read aloud. But within seconds, he intoned these words: "The game is done, I've won, I've won!"

With that, the class roared in exultation and Mr. Freda threw the book over his shoulder and ordered the radios turned back on to the postgame show.

It's in that spirit that on every October 16, at 3:14 PM, the precise time on Shea Stadium's scoreboard clock when Davey Johnson's fly ball settled into Jones' glove, a satisfying warmth overtakes me and I think how at that moment on that magnificent day my life and career were shaped, and I thank every member of that team for teaching us all that if you reach for the stars, you just might grab a handful.

Chapter 3
TO TELL THE TRUTH

When and where did it all begin for me? When did I decide I wanted to be a sportscaster?

Would you believe that it started for me when I was five years old?

I'm not sure if I really remember all of this or if I remember it because I've heard about it for years from family members, but my first broadcasting influence, if you will, was Bud Collyer, who was a popular television game show host in the 1950s and early '60s (*Beat the Clock, To Tell the Truth*). In those early days of rudimentary technology, the microphone was a long, narrow cylinder that was hooked around the neck of the show's host.

At the time, we had a Polaroid camera and the film for the camera came on a spool that loosely resembled the microphone Bud Collyer was using on his game show. When we ran out of film, my mom would tie a string around the spool and then tie it around my neck and I'd walk around, at the age of five, pretending I was Bud Collyer interviewing people, or Mel Allen shouting "How about that?" into my homemade "microphone."

Who can say if that experience at age five was an indication that I was destined to be a broadcaster? What I can say with certainty is that for me the defining moment, when it all came together and I decided this is what I wanted to do with my life, was when I was 12 years old.

While as a kid I was obsessed with the Mets, I also started to get interested in the New York Rangers. I needed something to occupy myself between baseball seasons and hockey fit in perfectly. So did basketball—I liked basketball, and I lived and died with the Knicks team of Willis Reed, Walt Frazier, and Bill Bradley—but for some of the same reasons I adopted the Mets I found myself attracted more to the Rangers than the Knicks. If I were to psychoanalyze it, I'd say it was because back then there was something about hockey that was against the grain. Most kids in my school, most kids my age in New York, were not hockey fans. It seemed everybody was a basketball fan. I wanted to do my own thing, and just like I attached myself to the Mets because most everybody else I knew was rooting for the Yankees, so too I followed the Rangers because most everybody else I knew was rooting for the Knicks.

My introduction to hockey came rather serendipitously. One night I was flipping the dial around on the radio and I inadvertently landed on a Rangers game. And after listening to only part of one period, listening to Marv Albert describe the game, I not only became a Rangers fan, I became sold on the business of sports broadcasting. All because of Marv! He made it so exciting, I thought to myself that was exactly what I wanted to do.

I didn't know very much about hockey, but with that one period I determined to learn more about the game. I discovered that after going through some tough years, the Rangers had turned the corner by 1966 and were a pretty good team. Because they were improving, they were getting more coverage in the newspapers and on radio and television, so that made it easier for me to follow them. Having already committed myself to follow the fortunes of a struggling young team like the Mets, I suppose I was looking for a winning team to follow, and the Rangers were it. They became my team.

I used to have passing thoughts that it would be great to be Mel Allen or Lindsey Nelson, Bob Murphy, or Ralph Kiner, broadcasting games of the Yankees or the Mets, but the idea of a career in sportscasting never crystallized in my mind until I heard Marv do that one period of hockey.

Here I am with Mets broadcasting legend Bob Murphy (center), who broadcast the Mets from their inception in 1962 until his retirement in 2003, and former Mets broadcaster Steve LaMar (left) in spring training 1983.

About a year later, in eighth grade, I had to fill out a questionnaire for high school and one of the questions was: What do you want to be when you grow up?

So I figured, let's put it in writing, go on record, make it official and declare it formally. I wrote that I wanted to be a sportscaster. From that moment on, I spent every waking moment in pursuit of my dream.

Once I was bitten by the sportscasting bug, I was consumed by an insatiable desire to succeed. When I attended games I got in the habit of taking a tape recorder with me and, when possible, practicing and trying to perfect my play-by-play style.

I have dozens of hockey tapes from those days, but very few of baseball, simply because the first time I tried doing play-by-play of a baseball game I said, "This is not easy." I didn't have any notes or statistics in front of me. What, I wondered, do I do between pitches? Hockey is more mechanical than baseball. The pace of hockey is faster than baseball, so even if there isn't a lot of scoring in hockey there's always action to describe. In baseball you have to learn how to handle the slow pace and the gaps when the ball is not in play.

I find that baseball, especially on the radio, is the toughest sport to do. It's such an art to broadcast baseball on radio and the greatest responsibility in sports broadcasting.

I digress here to offer this bit of advice to aspiring young sportscasters. Even though your dream may be to be the voice of the New England Patriots or the Los Angeles Lakers or the Montreal Canadiens or the St. Louis Cardinals, or your goal is to concentrate on football or baseball or basketball, or to cover the Olympics or the Kentucky Derby, the wise thing is to start out being conversant with all sports so as to make yourself employable in all of them.

I pass that advice along despite the fact it's advice I never heeded myself.

As short-sighted as it was, my biggest goal, my entire focus, my passion, was to broadcast the games of my beloved New York Mets and/or New York Rangers. Talk about putting all your eggs in one big basket!

I never broadcast a boxing match or a horse race or a track and field meet or a golf tournament. I worked only a handful of basketball games, all of them for my college radio station, and only one football game. One!

Benjamin N. Cardozo High School in Bayside, which I attended, didn't have a football team and neither did my college, Queens College, so even though I became the sports director of the Queens College radio station, I never had the opportunity to broadcast a football game in high school or college.

In 1975, the Queens College women's basketball team was scheduled to play a game in Madison Square Garden against Immaculata College, which was going to be the first intercollegiate women's game ever played at the Garden, and we were going to carry it on the college radio station. At the time, radio station WNYC, the New York municipal station, was carrying CUNY (City University of New York) basketball games, so a few of us connected with the Queens College station convinced WNYC to carry the Queens-Immaculata women's game. They did, and I shared the play-by-play with the regular WNYC announcer and it apparently went over pretty well. That was my first huge broadcasting thrill; a game that people would be able to hear on a real radio station—and from the Garden, no less. I will never forget the date: February 22, 1975.

The following summer, I got a call from the person that produced CUNY sports on WNYC. They wanted to do a football game between the New York City Police Department and the Atlanta Police Department in Atlanta, and they asked me to do the play-by-play, which I thought was a big deal because I got to travel. (Years later I would come to realize that travel is drastically overrated.) I didn't know any of the players and I had no idea how to do a football game, but I talked to some guys that had experience doing football on radio and I came up with a rudimentary depth chart, in various colors, to distinguish the New York team from the Atlanta team and the offense from the defense.

The game was played on a high school field on a Friday night, and it poured rain. I mean it was like broadcasting a game being played in a monsoon, and by the second half the notes I had made in my preparation all got washed out, the colors running into one another and eventually fading so that I couldn't read them. I had no idea which players were doing what. It got so bad, I was making up names, like characters from *The Honeymooners,* "There's Wedemeyer fading back to pass."

Nobody picked up on what I was doing because nobody cared. There was nobody sitting in the stands, no crowd noise, no yard markers, I knew none of the players, and what little information I had was washed away by the rain. And there undoubtedly was no audience. After that pleasant experience, I decided I was never going to rival my idol Marv Albert as a football announcer.

I didn't go to broadcasting school or study with a speech therapist. I don't recommend following my lead to any young person, male or female, looking to get into sports broadcasting. I was fortunate and just seemed to be in the right place at the right time. I tell young people today that if you want to learn to speak, you listen; if you want to learn to write, you read. I always had that awareness, not so much who I wanted to emulate, but I tell youngsters if you have an announcer that you're bent on imitating a little, that's fine. That's like training wheels. If that's what makes you comfortable, learning the pace of the game, whether its baseball or hockey or basketball, and you find yourself sounding like Marv Albert or Mel Allen or Vin Scully, don't worry about that. It's not that you're imitating them for fun, or to mimic them, you're just using it as a device to get comfortable with pacing.

One lazy summer day in late August 1967, when I was 13, my friends and I were sitting around just killing time, nothing to do, and I said, "Let's start a fan club for Marv Albert." My friends said okay, and I said, "We really should get his permission." So since it was my idea, I took it upon myself to reach out to Marv and ask for his permission to start his fan club. I decided the best thing to do was to try reaching him at radio station WHN, where he was working. I called the station and told the switchboard operator in my high-pitched adolescent voice, "Can I maybe somehow speak to Marv Albert, please?"

The next thing I knew, I heard that familiar and unmistakable voice. "Hello!"

I was so tongue-tied hearing that voice that it took me several seconds to speak and make any sense, but eventually I got around to telling Marv that my friends and I wanted to start a fan club for him. He was

Eventually I'd end up working with greats like Marv Albert (center) and Marty Glickman (right). (Photo: George Kalinsky)

unbelievable. He embraced the idea wholeheartedly. He sent us a bunch of autographed glossy photographs that we could offer to prospective members, to whom we charged an admission fee of 25¢. When we returned to school we paid some kid to mimeograph a newsletter that we distributed to our members. We were so proud of it that I sent one to Marv, but in truth it was kind of sloppy and obviously amateurish. To his everlasting credit, Marv never commented on how unprofessional the newsletter was. Instead, he said, "The next time you do a newsletter, send me the handwritten manuscript and I'll have someone type it up and print it here at the station."

"Really!"

That's how I first got to know Marv, and from that day on he became a mentor, a benefactor, and a friend. In the early '70s, when I was still in high school, I had season tickets for the Rangers—$4.50 a game, 41 home games, $184.50 for the whole season, which I afforded by working that summer as a wagon boy at Waldbaums. My seat was not too far from where Marv broadcast the games. Madison Square Garden hung up a gondola in the last row of the building that housed the radio broadcast booth, and Marv had to walk right past my seat on his way to the booth. Often, he would stop by and hand me the press notes for that night's game. It was a nice and considerate gesture by Marv, and it made me feel like I was important.

At the time, my goal was to be a hockey broadcaster and it was hockey in which I put the majority of my early broadcasting energy. I guess in the back of my mind I figured I might have a faster path to success in hockey than if I went after something that everybody else was going after, which was a baseball play-by-play job. While I still thought of baseball as the ultimate in sportscasting, at the time I would have been content to be "the voice of the Rangers" for the remainder of my professional career.

As the years passed and I got more serious about wanting a career in sportscasting, Marv would critique my tapes. He was very detailed about it. He never sugarcoated anything or pulled any punches, all of it to my benefit. His criticisms were very particular and not in the least bit patronizing. He told me what was good and what wasn't, but he always encouraged me.

Marv was a powerful influence on me. Not only in my career, but in other important decisions in my life as well. I put such stock in him that whatever Marv suggested, I followed on faith.

When I graduated from high school and it was time to choose a college, the logical thing would have been for me to go to Queens College, an option I rejected. I felt it would have been like going to 13th grade, because everybody in my high school seemed to be going to Queens College. I wanted to experience something different, so I planned to go to a state school and I applied to several of them. But my dad got sick with what we now know as Alzheimer's disease, so it made sense for me to stay home and go to a CUNY (City University of New York) school. This allowed me to get a part-time job and help my family by earning some extra money.

I called Marv Albert and explained the situation to him and asked him if he knew which CUNY school was best for broadcasting. He suggested I go to Brooklyn College. If he had said go to Venus A&M, I probably would have. So I went to Brooklyn College and immediately got involved with the radio station, but after a semester I realized it was too far from home and the commute was wearing on me. I left Brooklyn College and transferred to, of all places, Queens College, which turned out to be the best thing I did both scholastically and in preparation for my career. At Queens, I got involved with the radio station and wound up getting valuable on-air experience and making important contacts in sports and broadcasting, as well as establishing friendships which endure to this day.

I always assumed that once I graduated from college, I would look to get any radio job I could doing baseball or hockey play-by-play in the minor leagues. I was fully expecting and completely willing to take the route that so many guys took, going out of town, working for some minor league team and trying to work my way back to New York. It never dawned on me that I wouldn't have to do that.

Almost everyone in the business I talked with told me that was probably going to be the route I would have to take, and I was prepared for that. I consider myself incredibly fortunate, though, in that I never had to leave New York; never worked a day out of New York. Who knows if I ever would have gotten back to New York if I had started my professional career in Podunk, in the Class A Armpit League.

Enter Marv Albert once again to save me from Podunk and the Armpit League!

Back in the day there was a rather progressive and ingenious concept called Sports Phone in which people could dial a number and get a pre-recorded one-minute sportscast with updates of scores and other breaking news. To do these reports they needed reporters, and since the idea was new and probably underfinanced, they hired young people, mainly college students or recent graduates that were looking to break into the broadcast business and would be available and willing to work part-time on weekend nights.

Heading up Sports Phone was a man named "Bullet" Bob Meyer, who was the track announcer at Yonkers and Roosevelt Raceway. He was also Marv Albert's statistician on Knicks and Rangers games. Meyer asked Marv if he knew of any college-aged kids who were looking for an entry-level position in broadcasting and Marv gave him my name. At the time, I was attending Queens College and working on the college radio station. One day I walked into the station's office and there was a message in my mailbox to call Bob Meyer.

At this point, the name Bob Meyer rang a bell, but I didn't immediately assume it was the Bullet, nor could I figure out why he would be calling me. As soon as he answered the phone, I had my answer.

"Are you the kid that used to call Marv Albert at WHN just before he went on the air?"

"No, I'm the guy who called him just after he went off the air!"

We both laughed, and I realized exactly to whom I was speaking. He told me that there was this start-up operation called SportsPhone, and that they were primarily looking for college-aged aspiring broadcasters, and that Marv had given him my name and told him that I would be a good fit. Of course, he would need to hear a tape of my work, and I would have to come in for an interview, but when I hung up the phone, I couldn't help but think that I had just been given a huge opportunity, thanks to Marv Albert.

The interview went well, Bob liked my tape, and I was hired to handle the on-air sports reports on weekend evenings. My compensation was five dollars an hour, which to a 21-year-old in 1975 represented righteous bucks. The job stood on its own as an entry-level position into broadcasting, but it was also a tremendous training ground. We had 59 seconds to record a report, which became valuable experience for when I eventually handled network radiocasts or television work where you had to be off the air at a precise time. The other thing we needed to be was accurate; not only because it's generally a good idea to get it right, but because if you didn't, there was a chance you would hear from some potentially unsavory characters.

A huge chunk of SportsPhone's clientele were gamblers. Big gamblers. Remember now, this was before all-sports radio, and before Al Gore invented the internet. We were a gamblers' lifeline. It wasn't enough to be accurate when identifying the winning team, the score needed to be 100 percent correct as well, because those who wagered were concerned with the point spreads. One wrong score and an announcer could find himself in the witness protection program. Thankfully, I never had to deal with anything like that. But occasionally, if a lead changed hands late in a game, an irate caller to the office would wonder if we had our information right. Those could be somewhat unsettling conversations, but the bottom line is that someone was listening. To a rookie broadcaster, just knowing that you had a captive audience was a thrill in itself.

Oops

Anyone who has earned a living speaking into a microphone has had moments he or she would like to forget, moments and utterances they would take back if they could. I'm no exception. Here are my six (hopefully there will never be a seventh) most embarrassing moments as a sportscaster.

1. I was fortunate that the subject of my first "professional" interview was a terrific person, otherwise there might never have been a second. This occurred in 1973, early in my freshman year at Queens College. Lou Carnesecca, the legendary St. John's basketball coach, had left college to try his hand in the pros as coach of the New York Nets of the ABA (American Basketball Association).

Through WQMC, the college radio station, I had received accreditation to cover a Nets game in the Nassau Coliseum on Long Island. The Nets had been hit with a rash of injuries, so to fill out their roster they signed a few free agents, including a player named George Bruns (that's B-R-U-N-S) who had been teaching at Nassau Community College, practically across the street from Nassau Coliseum.

After the game I took my tape recorder into the Nets dressing room and approached Carnesecca. My first question to him—the first question I had ever asked a professional player or coach—was, "What did you think of George BURNS tonight?"

Had I posed the question to Gracie Allen or Harry Von Zell (kids, ask your parents about them), it might have worked, but this had fiasco written all over it. Luckily for me, Louie is a sweetheart—was then and still is today—and instead of belittling me or calling attention to my ignorance, with a warm smile he sensed my panic and politely corrected me, acknowledging the legendary entertainer I mistakenly referred to, and we moved on. I haven't forgotten Lou's grace, understanding, compassion, and patience with a college kid he didn't even know.

2. Chuck Tanner, former manager of the Pittsburgh Pirates, Chicago White Sox, Oakland A's, and Atlanta Braves, had a reputation for being one of the nicest people in Major League Baseball. Leave it to me to severely test that reputation.

It happened in 1978 after a game between the Mets and Tanner's Pirates in Shea Stadium. With the score tied 2–2 in the eighth inning, the Mets brought in rookie Mardie Cornejo to pitch. With one out, he walked Omar Moreno, who promptly stole second. That forced the Mets to issue an intentional walk to Dave Parker. Moreno and Parker then executed a double steal and both scored on an error by third baseman Bobby Valentine, and the Mets lost 4–2.

After the game, I took my trusty tape recorder and joined the press contingent in the visiting manager's office. Holding the microphone in Tanner's face, I politely asked him if he noticed anything in Cornejo's delivery that made him think the rookie would be easy to steal on.

Somewhat sheepishly, but calmly, Tanner replied, "Well, we saw a few things…." and left it at that. But I didn't. Feeling that at age 24 I needed to display my inner Mike Wallace, I pressed on. "Such as?" I queried. Suddenly the nicest man in baseball shot me an angry glare that could melt my microphone and snapped, "That's *our* business."

At that point, without a clever rejoinder at my immediate disposal and with my kneecaps aching from knocking into one another, I turned away with my mike still in Tanner's face and noticed that every pair of eyes in that room, most of them veteran baseball writers and radio reporters, was fixed on me. Two or three times I looked back at Tanner and he was still staring me down. Sensing that this cold war could continue for hours, I mouthed something clever like "Okay," and that was the cessation of hostilities. Early in my career and at a very young age I had learned a valuable lesson: it's okay to ask a probing follow-up question, but don't expect a manager, coach, or player to give away state secrets, especially when he doesn't know you and you look like you walked into the wrong room on your way to study hall.

Some 30 years later, I was in Pittsburgh with the Mets, and in the press room I ran into Tanner, who by then was still in baseball as a scout. We chatted and I reminded him of that incident in Shea Stadium's visiting manager's office three decades earlier. We both had a good laugh about it, and after all those years Chuck Tanner returned to being the nicest man in baseball.

3. I view this embarrassing moment as a badge of honor. Phil Rizzuto—"The Scooter"—was a New York legend, first as a Hall of Fame shortstop for the New York Yankees in the 1940s and '50s and later as a broadcaster for his former team. As a broadcaster he frequently employed the word "huckleberry" as an all-purpose term to describe someone he didn't like, was mad at, or simply was needling good-naturedly. I like to believe I was in the latter group when he branded me with the famed Rizzuto honorific.

This was before I began working for the Mets. I was covering a Yankees home game and, as I often did in the pre-Internet age, I was also monitoring the Mets game on my transistor radio.

Rizzuto walked by, spotted me with my ear to my transistor, and asked me what the score was.

"Three to two in favor of the Mets," I replied.

Rizzuto immediately became apoplectic.

"The Mets!" he shrieked. "You're listening to the Mets game? I thought you were listening to the Red Sox or the Orioles."

And then came his crowning achievement for all to hear.

"Holy cow! Can you believe this Huckleberry [there it was in all its glory, the dreaded-by-some, cherished-by-others renowned Rizzuto Huckleberry] listening to the Mets game in the Yankee Stadium press box?"

It was clear to one and all that now the Scooter was on stage, performing and playing it for laughs—and succeeding. Everyone in the press box had a good laugh, including me. It might have seemed embarrassing at the time, but through the years it has become a memory I will cherish forever. Phil Rizzuto called me a Huckleberry. Now to make my life complete, I have to figure out a way to get Don Rickles to call me a hockey puck.

4. Through the years I have prided myself on being pretty good at handling things on the air that are beyond my control. One night, however, that was not the case. During my talk show on radio station WFAN in the early 1990s, an open mike in the control room was bleeding into my headset and I couldn't hear my in-studio guests, even though they were seated only inches away from me.

Several times I used the "off air" talkback button to communicate with the control room and inform them of the problem and was told that they'd take care of it. I kept being told that the problem was solved, but nothing seemed to change. Consequently, my interview was a mess. I couldn't properly respond to what my guests were saying, owing to the ambient noise that kept leaking into my headset.

I finally lost my cool, and when we went to a commercial break, I stormed into the control room and screamed, "You've got a [bleeping] mike on in here and I can't hear my [bleeping] guests."

Without waiting for a response, I turned on my heels and went back into the studio, preparing to go back on the air. Suddenly someone from the control room burst frantically into the studio to tell me that the entire control room exchange, expletives and all, had gone out over the air, loud and clear. Not only were they unable to fix a relatively simple problem, now I was going to have to deal with irate listeners and an angry boss with my job possibly on the line.

Fortunately, I was able to dodge the bullet. I issued the necessary and proper apologies, and that was the end of it. No caller complained specifically about my language, although I did receive a letter scolding me for a lack of professionalism. None wrote in to report me to management. And apparently no one in management was listening at the time (I don't know if that was good or bad). Just like that the incident—but thankfully not my career—was over.

5. An escapade similar to the one at WFAN took place in Atlanta during the MSG Network telecast of a game between the New York Islanders and Atlanta Thrashers in November 2010.

It's customary, in order to conserve on expenses, for the station televising the game for the visiting team to hire some of the game's technical staff from the home city on a per-diem basis. Generally, this temporary help is very professional and efficient, but there are occasions when some of the hired help, to put it delicately, does not have a great deal of experience or simply are not as skillful as one would like.

On this particular night we encountered an abundance of technical issues making it clear we were in for a long and difficult evening.

During the first period there was a stoppage of play so I threw to commercial. At least I thought I did. While we were in the "break," my producer in the production truck was telling me in my headset what our problems and limitations were. My microphone was open so I could talk back to the producer. I was supposed to use the talkback button, which had the effect of killing the mic. Lazily, I failed to hit the talkback button so that my conversation with the producer went out over the air. With my frustration bubbling over at one point, I blurted for our audience to unintentionally hear, "Is it spring training yet?"

That wouldn't have been so bad if that was the end of it. It wasn't. A few seconds later the game was set to continue but we were still in commercial, or so I thought, which meant we would lose several seconds of live action, and that prompted me to say, "Let me know how the game turns out...not that I particularly care."

By that point I was so frustrated I just wanted to cut my losses and get out of Dodge as fast as I could. Unfortunately, the entire exchange went out over the air. Whoever was responsible for taking us from live action to commercial was asleep at the switch and my comments were heard by our viewers. I was devastated. It was just an offhand wise-guy comment. I actually did care about the game. What I didn't care about was the circus going on around me. Nevertheless I knew how it would be received. Islanders' general manager Garth Snow, my bosses at MSG Network, and many Islanders fans were livid, and they had a right to be. I thought I might even get fired, but when the powers-that-be learned of the technical problems we were having, they softened somewhat. It also helped that the episode became an instant sensation on YouTube, and that allowed viewers to see that the technical problems were real and not merely an excuse.

I admit I was totally to blame for the controversy and the entire sordid affair. I am a veteran, professional announcer and instead of lazily speaking into an open mike, I should have leaned forward and used the talkback. Had I done what I should have, the incident would have been avoided.

6. Ordinarily, one strives to be the best at something, but this one time I was pleased to be "the worst."

Ralph Kiner is a New York baseball treasure who has been a Mets broadcaster since their inception in '62. For many years, he hosted a popular postgame television show called *Kiner's Korner*.

Ralph and I partnered on Mets telecasts for eight seasons, which helped me forge a relationship with a Hall of Fame player and one of the nicest men I have known. So I was especially flattered when, during the late '90s, I was asked to be Ralph's final guest of the season on *Kiner's Korner*. For one who grew up watching the show, this was a seminal moment. There I was sitting next to the host on the famous set as the show opened with its iconic theme music.

When Kiner introduced me, I said, "You know, Ralph, this is a big thrill for me. I thought you had to have had a few hits, or a game-winning home run, or pitch a shutout to be on *Kiner's Korner*. What am I doing here?"

Instantly, there was a deadpan look on Ralph's face, but a mischievous twinkle in his eye and a tiny wrinkle of a smile at the corner of his mouth as he replied with engaging sarcasm, "Yeah, come to think of it, you're the worst guest we've ever had."

I couldn't help laughing. Neither could everyone else around the set and in the control room.

After watching Casey Stengel, Tom Seaver, Willie Mays, Hank Aaron, and countless other huge names in baseball history appear as guests on that show, on the same set and sitting in the same seat that I was occupying, joke or not, Ralph was right. I was easily the worst guest he ever had; and I was damned proud of it.

Chapter 4
BREAKING IN

I'm not certain how many games I had watched at Shea Stadium from my "reserved" seat in Section 1, Row 1 by the time I began with Sports Phone in 1975. Based on my estimate that I attended between 20 to 30 games a season, I figure I had seen from 200 to 300 Mets games from my usual perch, but I had never been privileged to gain entry to the charmed circle, the precious inner sanctum, the press box, until Sunday, June 20, 1976. The date is etched indelibly in my consciousness, mainly because I'm anal about remembering significant dates in my history with the Mets, but partly because it happened to be Father's Day.

I'd been assigned to cover the game between the Mets and the Giants, which meant phoning in periodic updates on the status of the game. I was a wide-eyed, 22-year-old kid, green as the Shea Stadium grass, awestruck and intimidated by my surroundings, and feeling somewhat overwhelmed and overmatched. But I was a professional.

The Mets had provided me with credentials that granted access not only to the press box but also to the press room. There I could partake of a sumptuous buffet brunch at no charge and be on par (at least theoretically) and rub elbows with the veteran, crusty baseball writers whose bylines were so familiar to me. It was great. These were my heroes and role models in the broadcast industry.

As a young broadcaster I got to meet tons of interesting people. For instance, The Fonz, Henry Winkler, at Shea Stadium with the Happy Days *cast for a softball game against the Mets' wives.*

I dressed in my Sunday best, suit and tie, and arrived very early in the press room where there was a small gathering of my "peers." But I knew none of them, so I took a seat at a table by myself. I was minding my own business, trying to look like I was a regular and belonged in this environment, when Bob Murphy—one of my idols—walked in. Although I recognized him instantly, I didn't know Murph and he certainly didn't know me. I heard someone on the other side of the room shout, "Hey, Bob, how are you doing? Good to see you."

As Bob acknowledged the greeting and started to respond it flashed through my mind that now I was going to hear what this jolly guy sounds like off the microphone, in real life.

"Well hiya there and a happy Father's Day to you," Bob replied, sounding exactly like he did on the air; the same intonation, the same cadence, the same lilt in his voice, just like he was opening a broadcast.

By working for Sports Phone I was able to get credentials to cover games for all of the New York teams—the Mets and Yankees, the Knicks and Rangers—and that in turn enabled me to do a little freelance work for WCBS radio covering some baseball, basketball, and hockey, and also covering the Queens College women's basketball team, which went to the national tournament a few times when I was in school.

There are two people in sports I revere because of how well they treated me when I was young, impressionable, and just starting out in the business. They are Al Arbour, the longtime and enormously successful coach of the New York Islanders, and Joe Torre, whom I got to know in his first job as a manager with the Mets, some two decades before he became the manager of the Yankees.

I was still in college when I first dealt with these two men and both of them treated me like I had been on the beat for 10 or 15 years. That's consistent with who they are. They weren't giving me any special consideration. To their credit they were merely treating me with the same respect as every other reporter, young or old. That's just how they operate.

That part-time gig with Sports Phone jump-started my broadcasting career. I haven't worked at anything else since. Two years after starting with Sports Phone, and less than a year out of college, I was hired to do morning sports reports for radio station WHN. Ironically, WHN was where my broadcast mentor and benefactor Marv Albert was working when I first met him, and which, a few years later, would become the Mets' flagship station.

It was while I was working at WHN that my youthful idolatry of teams and their components collided head-on with my attempts at maintaining an air of professionalism. One incident in particular provided me with the supreme test of my newly required impartiality.

On June 15, 1977, on what came to be known as the "Midnight Massacre," the Mets traded Tom Seaver, "The Franchise," their best player, a nine-time All-Star, four-time 20-game winner, and three-time Cy Young Award recipient, to the Cincinnati Reds for four players: pitcher

Some of the WHN family: starting at the bottom right and moving clockwise there's WHN program director Ed Salamon, Tommy Lasorda, disc jockey Del DeMontreux, Joe Torre (he and Lasorda were guest disc jockeys in 1979), and me.

Pat Zachry, infielder Doug Flynn, and outfielders Steve Henderson and Dan Norman.

For weeks, there had been rumors that Seaver was looking for a lucrative new contract that the club thought was exorbitant. The Mets leaked stories to the press branding Seaver selfish, a malcontent, and a money-grubber, which prompted Seaver to ask to be traded. In addition, Seaver was an activist with the Major League Baseball Players Association, and his involvement with the union irritated the Mets' stodgy and conservative chairman of the board, M. Donald Grant.

I was told by Joe Torre and Ed Kranepool, in separate conversations years later, that when the Mets were negotiating the trade of Seaver, they were playing the Dodgers and Reds against each other. Torre and Kranepool both said that the Dodgers had a package on the table that would have included pitcher Rick Rhoden, infielder Lee Lacy, and outfielder Pedro Guerrero for Seaver, but the Mets turned it down and took the Reds' offer instead. Mets general manager Joe McDonald denied to me those accounts of the Dodgers' offer.

In retrospect, the Mets would have been better served had they taken the Dodgers' offer, but at the time Lacy was a journeyman infielder of 29, Rhoden was only 24 and had won a handful of games in the major leagues, and Guerrero was a 21-year-old minor leaguer who was still several years away from becoming a consistent 30–home run, 100-RBI star.

Apparently, Seaver met with Grant and they worked out an agreement that would enable Seaver to remain a Met. On Sunday, June 12, Seaver beat the Astros in Houston 3–1, with a five-hitter. Although the Mets were mired in last place in the National League East, Seaver raised his record to 7–3.

The Mets left Houston and flew to Atlanta, where they beat the Braves on Monday, June 13, their third straight win, but then they lost the next day.

Wednesday, June 15, was the final game of the Mets' seven-game road trip. It also was the major league trading deadline. That morning, Seaver received a call from a friend in New York who told him that the day's New York *Daily News* was running a column by Dick Young saying that Seaver's wife, Nancy, was envious of Ruth Ryan, whose husband, Nolan, had been traded by the Mets and was now a big star with the California Angels and earning more money than Seaver.

Seaver was livid. He decided then and there that he no longer wanted to be a Met and the trade with the Reds was consummated. Seaver would go from the National League East to the National League West and from a last-place team to the defending two-time World Series champions, or as someone would say, from the outhouse to the penthouse.

The Mets had a night game on Thursday, June 16. That morning, Seaver went to Shea Stadium to clear out his locker and meet the press. He came with a prepared statement, which he started to read. However, Seaver got emotional and couldn't get through it and so he gave it to broadcaster Spencer Ross to finish. Seaver's new team, the Reds, had that day off. Seaver would join them the following night, June 17, when the Reds opened a series in Montreal.

The Seaver trade hit home because it was a transition period for me. My personal feelings as a lifelong Mets fan were colliding with my role as a professional journalist. Seaver had been my idol growing up, but now I was 23 years old and I was working at WHN. A lot of that idolatry I had when I was younger had been peeled away so that now I could look at things a lot more objectively when it came to trades and understanding the reasons for them.

I don't mean to overdramatize it, but it forces you to grow up a little. As a kid you have this wide-eyed image of athletes, and then you're among them in a professional setting, and you have no choice but to change. You realize you have responsibilities that are a lot greater than waving a pom-pom. I understood that very early, but it was still a jolt of adulthood to see the guy you used to watch pitch from the upper deck when you were 13 go away and leave your favorite team in the lurch.

As a fan, I wasn't happy with the trade. Not only were the Mets losing Seaver, their biggest star, but they weren't getting anybody back that had anything close to Seaver's cachet. On another level, I was disappointed with the trade because I was just starting out in the business and figuring I had a good chance to cover, and get to know, this great pitcher that I had idolized since he joined the team when I was a kid. Then bang, he's traded. And to smack me in the face with the ultimate test of fan vs. reporter, I was assigned by my news director at WHN to take my tape recorder and go to the airport and try to get a comment from Seaver on his way to the gate to board the plane that would take him to Montreal.

At the airport, with my trusty tape recorder in hand, I followed Seaver to the gate, asking him questions like a seasoned reporter with one half of me, and the other half wanting to corral him by the neck and drag him back to Shea Stadium where I thought he belonged.

To make matters worse for the fan in me, in his first game as a Red in Montreal on Saturday, June 18, Seaver beat the Expos 6–0, with a three-hitter. He struck out eight, as well as contributing two hits and two RBI, and finished the season with 21 wins. The fan in me, however, was becoming increasingly irrelevant. Whether I felt like accepting it or not, I was now a professional, and the instincts of my youth yielded to my role as sports director of a 50,000 watt radio station. This new lot in life was certainly exciting, but not totally devoid of pitfalls.

I admit now that getting the job at WHN made me a little lazy. I was complacent because I was 23 years old, I had a gig in New York, and I was making decent money (I was single at the time). I knew that leaving town to take a minor league job in any sport would be taking a step back financially. Why, I reasoned, would I want to go out of town and try to work my way back to New York when I already had a job in New York? It didn't make any sense.

If there was anything that might have motivated me to go out of town it was to gain some experience doing play-by-play. Instead I rationalized that the way I could get to do play-by-play—which was my ultimate goal—without leaving New York was to establish a name, a recognition level, or even just credibility in New York. I figured that somebody would take a chance on me based on that, and that I could make the transition from reporter to play-by-play man. Perhaps I was naïve, although I did realize it was a gamble. But it was a gamble I thought was worth taking.

Timing, they say, is everything. But it doesn't hurt to have a little bit of luck mixed in. My luck was being in the right place at the right time, over which I had no control, or to put it another way, not being in the wrong place at the wrong time, over which I did have control.

By not taking the well-meaning advice of many to go out of town and try to work my way back to New York, I was able to hook on at WHN, which would prove to change my life. In 1983, WHN reacquired the rights to Mets' baseball and the station's format was a mix of Mets baseball and country music. However, I would soon be on the move.

I'd been at WHN for six and a half years when the station was sold in late 1983 and they eliminated sports, so I was out of a job. But within two weeks, with the help of some people—including Marv Albert who always seemed to be there for me—I landed two freelance jobs that more than compensated for being dropped by WHN.

My good fortune continued when the Mets made it to the World Series in '86. WHN wanted to ride the Mets' coattails and capitalize on their success and popularity, so they created a long pregame and

Working at WHN also gave me the opportunity to interview baseball legends like Billy Martin.

postgame show for the postseason that they called *Mets Extra*. The shows were hosted by a broadcaster named Dave Cohen (no relation to Gary) and the extremely popular former Met, Rusty Staub.

The shows were designed to run only for the '86 postseason, but they were so well-received that WHN decided that winter to make *Mets Extra* full-time pregame and postgame shows for the entire '87 season. When I heard about the plans, I thought that would be the perfect vehicle for me and, at the same time, maybe help me get my foot in the door as a potential play-by-play guy. I did get the gig to host *Mets Extra* and also return to do morning sports reports at WHN, which meant I was perfectly placed to chase my dream of becoming a play-by-play broadcaster for the Mets. Maybe I was going to have to use the back door instead of the front, but there was an entrance available nonetheless.

Thankfully, *Mets Extra*, which included a segment with the manager in the pregame show and call-ins from listeners on both the pregame and postgame shows, was a big success for a few years. But as the team began to decline, I started taking calls after games from irate fans that were frustrated with the state of the Mets and I had some rocky and tumultuous times. I had two choices: I could run from the controversy, be an apologist for the team and put myself in danger of being laughed off the air, or I could be honest and give my thoughts on why what was going on was going on. Even though the Mets had the right of approval of the announcers, I opted for the latter. I felt the master I was paid to serve was the radio station and, therefore, the fans. I never wanted to be a flag-waver or apologist for the team.

Eventually that got me into a little hot water with management, partly because I got along well with manager Davey Johnson, who was a rebel and would say things that would irk general manager Frank Cashen to no end. But in the end, Cashen, a decent and honorable man, and a former journalist himself, apparently let his journalism training rise above his commitment to the Mets, and I kept my job.

Meanwhile in spring '87, the company that owned and ran WHN decided it was going to turn the station into the first all-sports radio station ever. I was told I was going to be the host of the 7:00 PM to midnight shift in addition to continuing to do *Mets Extra*, a grueling schedule I would hold down for eight years.

Because of the new format, all of the WHN disk jockeys and many of its other employees were being phased out and a whole new staff would be taking over for what was to become radio station WFAN.

The changing of the guard took place in two separate studios at 3:00 PM on July 1, 1987. In one studio were all the WHN employees who were basically being put out of work, many of them in tears as WHN was signing off for the last time. I was in that studio kind of consoling them and mourning the loss of WHN.

Disk jockey Dan Taylor signed off for WHN, played Ray Price's "For the Good Times," and threw it to a commercial, at which time I left the WHN studio and tip-toed across into the WFAN studio. After the commercial, Suzyn Waldman, the first voice ever heard on WFAN, came on with an update followed by Jim Lampley, the host of WFAN's first call-in show. All the while I was in the booth and we were all hugging and high-fiving each other as we welcomed in the arrival of the new baby.

I stayed with WFAN until 1995. My big break, and my childhood dream, came true in '96 when I began doing play-by-play on Mets games along with Ralph Kiner, Fran Healy, and Matt Loughlin on cable TV for Sportschannel, which later became Fox Sports New York/MSG. In 2003, I moved to the radio booth, where I have shared space with Bob Murphy, Gary Cohen, Ed Coleman, Tom McCarthy, Wayne Hagin, and Josh Lewin.

I met Lindsey Nelson, but I never had anything to do with him professionally. He was no longer broadcasting Mets games when I came along. I have, however, worked with the Mets' two other pioneer broadcasters, Bob Murphy and Ralph Kiner, which to me was mind-boggling. When I stop to think about it and reflect on the odds of that coming to pass—being in sixth grade, playing stickball, listening to those guys every night, dreaming of doing what they were doing and not only doing it, but getting to do it with *them*—when I dwell on all of that, and the odds against that happening, it blows me away. It's overwhelming to me. It always has been.

I'm very respectful of that lineage. I want to get a large picture of those three pioneers, the first Mets broadcasters, and hang it in the radio booth at Citi Field. I've done things over the years, a kind of tribute to them, by using an inflection or a phrase that was unique to each of them, things I picked up by listening to them for so many years. Usually, it's subtle to the point of almost being subliminal. For instance, Lindsey

Here I am with Mets owner Fred Wilpon, shortly after he became part of the Mets ownership group and team president in 1980. I told him on that day that my goal was to someday become a Mets broadcaster. I am forever indebted to him for allowing me to realize my dream.

had a certain inflection when the Mets took the lead. I'll try to parrot that sometimes. It's not a cheap imitation, or a put-down, it's quite the opposite. It's a tribute, and it's a silent, understated homage. I've never called attention to it. Lindsey hasn't done Mets broadcasts since '78, so there are a lot of people listening today that have no idea what Lindsey Nelson sounded like. I'm doing that for me. It connects me and deepens the appreciation I have for what I'm doing and how we're all connected.

With Bob Murphy, it might be trying to replicate his home run call, or mimic his homespun humor and voice inflections, all with respect for his years of experience. Once I was doing a game with Murph, and Howard Johnson, who had been red hot at the time, got a 3–1 fastball right down the middle from the Giants Roger Samuels. HoJo had been locked in for weeks, and he turned that fastball around and drove it out of the park for a home run.

I commented on the air to Murphy, "How could you throw Howard a fastball in that situation the way he's been hitting?"

And without missing a beat, Murph said, "Yeah, it's like trying to sneak sunrise past a rooster."

With Ralph Kiner it might just be the way I tell a story. Ralph is simply one of nature's noblemen.

I have never heard anybody say a bad word about Ralph. I once saw a waiter spill a whole tray of drinks on him and it didn't tick him off. The only time I ever saw Ralph get even the slightest bit irked was one time when we were doing a game in San Diego. Ralph always used to have his cigar going in the booth, but eventually California passed a state ordinance that forbade smoking anywhere. Ralph had this cigar going and somebody came into the booth and very apologetically said, "Ralph, I'm really sorry, but there's a state ordinance now that says you can't smoke in public buildings."

Ralph just looked at the guy with a smirk and said, "You know, this used to be a great state."

That's as close to getting mad as I've ever seen Ralph.

Chapter 5
HEROES

My first Mets hero was Gil Hodges. I suppose the reason I was drawn to him was that I somehow knew that he had been a big name in his Brooklyn Dodgers days and also because in the only game I ever saw the Mets play at the Polo Grounds Hodges hit his last major league home run, helping the Mets beat the Cardinals. You have a tendency to remember things like that when you witness them at age eight.

I would come to idolize Hodges even more after he returned to manage the Mets in 1968 and then lead them to victory over the heavily favored Baltimore Orioles in the '69 World Series, which to my mind is the greatest sports story in New York City history. (Am I biased in that opinion? Of course, I am.)

I regret I never got to know Hodges or Casey Stengel; never got to meet either one of them. The first baseball player I ever met was Wes Westrum, who had played for the New York Giants and joined the Mets as a coach in '64. A year later, he became interim manager of the Mets when Stengel suffered a fractured hip, then took over the reins when Stengel retired. Westrum was replaced as Mets manager by Hodges.

My dad grew up in Corona, Queens, not far from where Shea Stadium would eventually sit. Across the Grand Central Parkway from Shea was a hotel called the Stadium View Inn, which was a kind of charcoal-colored building that players would stay at from time to time. Some even stayed there for the entire season because it was convenient. The hotel had a barber shop, and after my family moved from the Bronx to Queens, my dad would take me there for my haircuts because he knew Leo the barber, who was also from Corona.

One time we went to the barber shop and Leo the barber introduced me to this tough-looking, stocky man who turned out to be Wes Westrum, the manager of the Mets. I was 11 years old and, at the time, meeting him was the biggest thrill of my life. I remember him being a very nice man.

Once the Mets arrived and I began following them, except for Gil Hodges, my favorite Mets were not the veterans like Richie Ashburn, Gus Bell, Frank Thomas, and Roger Craig. Instead I drifted to the younger players that came along after I became a fan, guys like Rod Kanehl, Larry Bearnarth, and my No. 1 favorite, Ron Hunt. I felt I had a kinship with guys like that. It was like we were growing up together.

What attracted me to Hunt was that he was a hustler and a hard-nosed player who would do anything to win, including getting hit by a pitch. He was plunked 41 times in four seasons with the Mets. He later led the National League in HBP in his last seven seasons and is currently sixth on the all-time list having been hit 243 times in his career.

Hunt was the Mets' first homegrown starter, although he was signed originally by the Milwaukee Braves. However, he never played for Milwaukee and was purchased by the Mets after the '62 season. He joined the Mets the following year and was second in the National League Rookie of the Year voting to Pete Rose.

Somehow, I got to be friendly with Hunt years later, long after he left the Mets and retired from baseball. It began in 1987 (by then Ron had been retired for 13 years), when I was working at radio station WFAN. I learned that back home in his native Missouri, Hunt was involved with a program in which he sponsored a baseball team of youngsters, not necessarily to help them sign professional contracts but to help them gain exposure to college coaches in order to get baseball scholarships. The kids stayed on his property, Ron's wife prepared meals for them, and they played on a field he had built on the property, a real "Field of Dreams."

I thought it was a noble experiment worthy of putting on the air. At the same time it was a chance for me to interview a former Met and one of my first baseball heroes, so I contacted him and set up an interview.

Getting to know him was hysterical. I soon learned that Ron couldn't do an interview without swearing. I called him and put him on the air live via the telephone. I was broadcasting in a studio, Ron was in his home, and my producer was on the other side of the glass in the control room. In both the studio and the control room was a "dump button," which the host in the studio or the producer in the control room could hit if a caller or guest said something you didn't want going out over the air. During the course of the interview, I recalled an incident in the mid-'60s when a Cardinals player named Phil Gagliano broke Hunt's collarbone in a collision at second base. I asked Hunt if he ever had any dialogue with Gagliano over the incident.

"Yeah," he said in his Missouri drawl. "He called me in the hospital to apologize and I told him he was full of [bleep]."

I started laughing, but all of a sudden it occurred to me that he had committed a no-no. I figured the guys in the control room caught it and hit the "dump button," but when I looked in there it was clear nobody was paying attention until they saw me staring. Then they hit the button, but I think it was too late. I think it went out over the air, but I never got any feedback from the station.

A year later, I talked the station into letting me participate in a Mets Fantasy Camp where I would have access to former Mets. I played ball during the day and at night I interviewed them on my call-in show, which we broadcast from the lobby of the hotel that was the headquarters for the camp's guests and instructors, one of whom was Ron Hunt. It was another chance to interview one of my old favorites.

In the course of the interview, I said, "It's obvious you love teaching baseball. Have you ever thought about doing it professionally? Why aren't you working in some team's minor league system, or even as a major league coach?"

"Basically," my hero replied, "because the pay is horse[bleep]!"

Gulp! Not again! Unfortunately, there was no dump button on site, so the only thing I could think of was to go to a commercial and hope that nobody heard what he said. As I did, I looked over at Hunt and the expression on his face told me that he probably did these things on purpose.

"Couldn't you have thought of another way to say what you said," I asked him off the air.

"Well," he replied, "horse[bleep] is horse[bleep], ain't it?" He was smiling, that rascal.

My relationship with Hunt occurred long after he had retired. I never broadcast a game he played for the Mets. If I had, we probably never would have formed the bond we did. Once I began working as a journalist, even after I was employed by the Mets as a member of their broadcast team, I diligently sought not to socialize with players. It's a hard enough job when you're not colored by feelings for those you cover. Sometimes on the road you might have lunch with a guy, but never to the point of making specific dinner plans with a player. They have their lives and their friends and I have mine.

One time in Phoenix, I ran into Mike Piazza in the hotel restaurant. He was alone and I was alone and we wound up having lunch together, but it was never anything I would go out of my way to plan.

If I were to make an exception to that rule, it probably would have been with Gary Carter. The relationship between athlete and broadcaster can sometimes be adversarial, but that was never the case with the man everyone called "Kid." I can count on the fingers of one hand the number of players who have thanked me for something nice I said about them, and Carter was one of those players. He was one of the terrific people (not just athletes) that I've met and, even though we never really socialized, he is someone I felt close to.

I was devastated when Gary passed away. Although we knew it was coming, news of his death felt like a shot to the solar plexus. I took it personally. Not only was he cordial toward me—gracious and accommodating in our professional relationship—but we were also the same age and he was a central figure in one of the great triumphs of my favorite team. He was a man whose passion, personality, and performance consumed New York's baseball heart a generation ago.

When Carter died I found myself thinking back to December 10, 1984, the day the Mets acquired Gary from the Montreal Expos for Hubie Brooks, Mike Fitzgerald, Floyd Youmans, and Herm Winningham; the day the Mets "won" the '86 World Series by landing the missing piece of their puzzle. At the time of the trade two things raced into my mind. "Start the season tomorrow" and "Now we have our DeBusschere."

The Mets had gone through a terrible 10-year period in which they were below .500 eight times, but they had won 90 games in '84 and things were beginning to take shape. And then they got Carter, the final piece of the puzzle, just as the Knicks had done 16 years earlier. On December 19, 1968, the Knicks obtained Dave DeBusschere in a trade with the Detroit Pistons. He would be the missing piece of the puzzle that led to the Knicks' first NBA championship. Now we were hoping that lightning would strike again in New York sports.

In his first game as a Met, his first game at Shea Stadium in a Mets uniform, Carter got the crowd revved up with a sixth-inning double in which he went into second with a headlong dive. Then in the bottom of the 10th he hit a game-winning home run against Neil Allen of the Cardinals and heard an ear-splitting ovation from 46,781 grateful, adoring fans. The Mets won 98 games that season and finished second in the National League East, but they were coming on strong and lightning did strike again in New York sports the following year.

Upon joining the Mets, Carter brought with him a reputation for being almost too nice, too media savvy, and too upbeat to be believed. Some teammates and opponents resented him for that, teased him relentlessly, and behind his back suggested Gary's good-guy persona was disingenuous.

In his early days as a Met, I seemed to spend an inordinate amount of time looking for cracks in that persona, searching for the moment he would betray his reputation and morph into someone other than the person he presented publicly. I can say now, 20 years later and after observing him up close and personal in his five years as a Met, I never found that "other" Gary Carter. He never dropped his guard because there was no guard to drop. He was as genuine when the cameras, microphones, and notebooks disappeared as he was when they were in front of him.

I inadvertently and unwittingly tested Gary in '85, his first year as a Met. One Mets pitcher had a disarming propensity for giving up two-strike hits, and after one especially disheartening occasion, I privately sought out Carter for his opinion of this seemingly chronic lapse. As soon as the words had left my lips, I rued the question, realizing Gary might think I was baiting him into saying something negative about a teammate. I needn't have fretted.

Flashing his usual smile, Carter gave me a response that was honest, direct, and informative without being disloyal to his team or teammate.

"Well, as you know he doesn't throw all that hard," he said, "so if he doesn't locate his pitches with two strikes, he has a tendency to get hit."

Soon after that incident I began hosting *Mets Extra*. The postgame edition usually called for me to interview the star of the game for the Mets if they had won. When that star happened to be Carter, I was ecstatic. It meant I was going to get a subject who was affable, bright, entertaining, informative, and voluble. Normally, I had to ask him only one question and then let him talk…and talk….and talk. I believe to this day he holds the *Mets Extra* record for the lengthiest postgame interview, some 10 minutes. And I don't remember asking him more than one question.

In Carter's second year as a Met, he was instrumental in helping them win their second World Series. It was a triumph in some ways even more stunning than the team's first World Series championship in 1969, because they'd been one out away from elimination by the Boston Red Sox in Game 6. Two outs, nobody on base in the bottom of the 10th, the Mets down three games to two in the Series and 5–3 in the game as Carter came to bat. With his indomitable spirit driving his determination not to

Gary Carter celebrating with Ray Knight after the final out of the 1986 World Series. (AP Images)

be the final out of the World Series, he looped a single to left, giving the Mets life and starting the rally that would eventually lead to victory, and Game 7, and ultimately to a world championship.

That's the hit that many Met fans first recall when they reflect on Carter's days in New York, but there's another one that comes to mind for me, one that tells you a lot about his pride and professionalism. Eleven days before the rally-inducing hit against the Red Sox, the Mets and Houston Astros played Game 5 of the National League Championship Series at Shea Stadium, with the series tied at two games a piece. The fifth game was tied at 1–1 in the bottom of the 12th inning. Wally Backman was at second base, representing the winning run, as Carter faced Astros reliever Charlie Kerfeld. Earlier in the series, in Game 3 at Shea, Gary hit a comebacker to the mound against Kerfeld, who mockingly showed Carter the ball as he threw Gary out at first base.

The bespectacled Kerfeld was a fun, excitable chap, but you don't show up an opponent that way, particularly one with Carter's credentials, and think it won't come back to haunt you. Kid made sure that it did.

By the time he faced Kerfeld in Game 5, Carter was struggling badly. He was just 1-for-21 in the series, and 0-for-4 in the game, but with a chance to get even with the Astros pitcher and give the Mets the series lead, Gary came through. He hit a ground ball through the middle into center field for a base hit, scoring Backman with the winning run, and putting the Mets one win away from the National League pennant. The next day in Houston, Gary Carter caught 16 excruciating innings in the Mets' epic win, enabling them to face the Boston Red Sox in the World Series.

That hit against Kerfeld was, to me, what Carter was all about as a player and a person. He could have ripped Kerfeld publicly after the pitcher's antics in Game 3, but he didn't. Instead, Gary took the high road, and when he had his chance for revenge, despite being stuck in an awful batting slump, he found the resolve to come through with one of the biggest hits in franchise history. That, in part, is what made him special.

To those New Yorkers who were teenagers in '86, Carter's death possibly caused you to come to grips with the end of your childhood just as an earlier generation dealt with the end of theirs in 1980 with the assassination of John Lennon. Curiously, I often thought of Keith Hernandez and Gary Carter as the John Lennon and Paul McCartney of the '86 Mets, two people with disparate personalities who combined to make beautiful music, in this case on a baseball diamond.

My mind's eye can easily imagine Hernandez, with his acerbic wit, writing, "How Do You Sleep?," and I feel reasonably certain that Carter was a proponent of "Silly Love Songs."

And what's wrong with that?

The 10 Most Important/Influential/Iconic/Indispensable Persons in the Mets First Half Century:

1) Tom Seaver: He was called "The Franchise" for a reason. From his rookie season in 1967 through his entire 12 years (in two hitches) with them, the Mets looked different, played better, and usually won when he pitched. He gave them respectability—along with 198 wins, four 20-win seasons, 10 All-Star selections, and three Cy Young Awards—and made them relevant. In his first two years, prior to the World Series championship season of 1969, when he was on the mound there was a seriousness about the Mets, and a respect from their opponents, that we had not seen before. The championships, numbers, awards, and that plaque in Cooperstown tell the rest of the story.

2) Keith Hernandez: What Seaver was to the Mets' first championship era, Hernandez was to the second. He was the soul of a terrific team that should have won more than it did. He's the first man I ever saw play first base as though he was a middle infielder. Just as Seaver changed the culture of the Mets when he was a rookie, so did Hernandez when he came from the Cardinals in a 1983 trade. He was a leader, a clutch hitter, and a defensive genius. And he even dated Elaine Benes.

3) Dwight Gooden: For the first two years of his career, it looked as if the Mets had the closest thing to a perfect pitcher. He won 41 games before his 21st birthday! Think about that for a moment (Cy Young, who won 511 games, didn't win his first one until he was 23). Although many lament the pitcher that should have been, the one that was remains second to Tom Seaver on the Mets' all-time list in wins and strikeouts. Furthermore, he was the greatest drawing card in franchise history. Games that he started at Shea Stadium were events, often transcending even the games themselves.

It was my pleasure to welcome Gooden into the Mets Hall of Fame in August 2010. (Photo: Marc S. Levine, New York Mets)

4) Gil Hodges: It might seem strange that I revere someone I never knew, but that's how strongly I feel about his place in Mets history. Even as a 14-year-old I could tell that everything changed as soon as he became the manager. The minute he showed up for spring training in 1968, the joke was over. The Mets were now a meritocracy, and even though they finished the season in ninth place that year, it was evident they were in business. What he accomplished in 1969 speaks for itself—but what he might have accomplished had he lived past April 1972 remains a wistful memory. He had major input into personnel decisions, and his death, in my opinion, set the franchise back a decade. And just for fun, he was an original Met who hit the first home run in franchise history.

5) Mike Piazza: The Mets were a nice little team in 1998 until Piazza was made available by the Florida Marlins almost immediately after they obtained him from the Dodgers. Like Gary Carter a decade earlier, he was the missing piece to the puzzle and the minute he arrived the Mets went from mediocre to marquee. They had never had a hitter like Piazza before he arrived, and they haven't had one since he left. The hardest ball I ever saw hit by a Met was a home run Mike hit at Shea Stadium off Ramiro Mendoza of the Yankees that sailed over the tent beyond the left-field bullpen and landed about 10 minutes later.

6) Casey Stengel: The George Washington of the Mets and the Father of the Franchise. He was the centerpiece of one of the great anomalies in sports. The worst team in baseball was actually one of the most beloved teams in New York sports history, all because of Stengel, the Ol' Perfessor. He played the role of clown, bandleader, entertainer, and for some of his younger players, teacher. Even in his seventies, he was the last one to bed after a night game—keeping "his writers" up into the wee hours with stories that couldn't be printed and quotes that were—and the first one up the next morning. There is not a marketer or public relations person in all of sports who ever could do what Stengel did, selling his brand-new team that almost from day one outdrew the firmly established and entrenched champion Yankees.

7) Darryl Strawberry: Linked forever with Dwight Gooden, the immediate temptation is to consider the career he should have had before the one that he did have, yet despite the turmoil and controversy, he's the all-time franchise leader in home runs and anticipation. The latter was sometimes rewarded with the former, but from the moment he was selected as the first-overall pick in the 1980 free agent draft, Mets fans closely followed his ascent through the minor leagues. Strawberry was one of those rare, special players who, when he came to bat, forced you to stop whatever it was you were doing and give him your undivided attention.

8) Frank Cashen: The greatest general manager in franchise history, he inherited not much more than an expansion team when he took over in January 1980, charged with rebuilding the Mets practically from scratch. It wasn't smooth sailing at first. He was found guilty of a terrible decision to leave a still useful and iconic Tom Seaver exposed in the free agent compensation pool, leading to Seaver's acrimonious departure in 1984. Nevertheless, one cannot do a better job of taking a struggling ballclub and building it into a champion with sound drafts and wise trades. It's noteworthy that even with the resources of the National League franchise in New York at his disposal, Cashen built the 1986 World Series champions without signing a free agent.

9) David Wright: Among the handful of best position players ever developed by the Mets, Wright is five times as much the person as he is the player. It's mind-boggling what he does on a daily basis as the unofficial spokesman of the players. On any team-related issue, good or bad, there's David at his locker surrounded by writers, radio and television reporters, cameras and microphones, patiently answering questions and addressing issues in a polite, intelligent, and respectful manner that speaks volumes about his upbringing. By the time his Mets career is over, he should own a chunk of their offensive record book.

10) Lindsey Nelson/Bob Murphy/Ralph Kiner: I know, that's three people, not one, but it's my book and my rules and, to me and thousands like me, for 17 years they formed the original Mets broadcasting trio on radio and television and carried it off as though they were one. For the first generation of Mets fans, they were the sounds of summer, practically a member of our family. If I was at a game at Shea Stadium that the Mets won in dramatic fashion, I wondered all the way home how Lindsey, Bob, and Ralph called it from the booth, and how excited they got. They helped instill in me the passion that led me to take up occupancy in what will always be *their* broadcast booth. For that, I am forever indebted.

Chapter 6
FALLEN HERO

I once asked Cleon Jones if there was a time in 1973 when he thought the Mets had no shot to win the pennant.

"Yeah," he replied in his inimitable way. "Spring training!"

Maybe it was a function of being 19 years old, naïve, and ever unrealistically hopeful, but I was somewhat less pessimistic than Cleon. I actually thought the Mets brought a pretty good team to camp that spring: a pitching rotation headed by the big three of Tom Seaver, Jerry Koosman, and Jon Matlack, with Tug McGraw in the bullpen; Cleon Jones, Bud Harrelson, Jerry Grote, Ed Kranepool, and Wayne Garrett, all who had been through the championship run only four years earlier; and three key additions since the championship season of 1969: veterans Rusty Staub and Felix Millan, and second-year first baseman John Milner, a promising young left-handed hitter coming off an impressive rookie season.

For reasons known mainly to the baseball gods, the Mets had stumbled in the three years after their championship season. Were they complacent? Did they suddenly lose their hunger? Did they mistakenly assume they could ride the momentum of 1969 and continue to win by simply going through the motions? Did the rest of the National League suddenly take the formerly ragamuffin Mets seriously for the first time and approach them differently and more determinedly?

Whatever the reason, the Mets finished in third place in '70, six games out of first, and in fourth place in '71, 14 games behind. In '70, they were tied for first on September 14 and proceeded to lose 10 of their final 15 games. In '71, they were in first place on June 9 and lost 59 of their last 110 games. The two seasons were a wake-up call, a painful reminder of how fleeting fame and success can be. What happened in the spring of '72 was a catastrophe that would change the course of the Mets for decades.

News traveled much slower in '72 than it does today. There was no Internet back then, no smartphones. It was Easter Sunday, April 2, and spring training was winding down, which meant I was getting excited for the start of the new baseball season only a few days away. I was in my room, talking on the telephone with a friend that afternoon when my dad came in and said somberly, "Gil Hodges just died of a heart attack."

I was devastated. I was in shock. I could remember back only a few years earlier and the completely different feelings I'd had when I heard that Hodges was coming to the Mets to be their manager. The Mets had just completed their sixth consecutive disastrous season, finishing in last place in the National League for the fifth time with a record of 61–101. Less than two months after the last game of the '67 season, on November 27, came the announcement that the Mets had completed a deal to bring Gil Hodges back home from Washington, where he had been managing the equally pitiful Senators, to take control of the Mets. The Mets sent pitcher Bill Denehy to Washington as compensation. Hodges had actually been hired on October 11, 1967, but it wasn't until the following month that the deal became official.

Bringing Hodges back wasn't a great surprise. The Mets had relieved Wes Westrum as manager with 11 games remaining and the rumors that Hodges was the man they wanted to succeed Westrum had been around for weeks, so we were all clued in on the change. Still, I was ecstatic. Even at age 14, I knew about the history of Gil Hodges in New York, so from that standpoint alone I thought getting him was a great move. I knew that as a manager for five years with the Senators, he improved them every year. I was too young to remember Hodges as a Brooklyn idol. I always thought of Gil as a Met.

You could feel the excitement when it was official that Hodges was returning to New York. For me the excitement stemmed from what I started to see and read during the '68 season, the way his players talked about him with awe and reverence, which was in direct contrast to his predecessor. Wes Westrum was portrayed as a pleasant country bumpkin, which fed into the stereotype of the Mets as being cartoonish. Gil was anything but cartoonish. Even a 14-year-old could see that.

Hodges didn't perform any miracles in his first year as manager of the Mets, but he did change the culture and perception of the team and he did make them better. The '68 Mets won 73 games, 12 more than the previous season, and moved up a notch in the standings to ninth place.

The miracle would come a year later when Hodges' Mets stunned the baseball world by winning the World Series. That skyrocketed

Gil Hodges looks on during Game 2 of the 1969 World Series on October 12, 1969.
(AP Images)

Hodges into legendary and iconic status as a manager and enabled him to withstand temporary setbacks in the two following years.

By all accounts, with Hodges in command the Mets were in good hands for the future. But suddenly on April 2, 1972, that promising future was gravely in doubt with word out of Florida that the Mets' strong, silent leader had been felled by a heart attack two days before his 48th birthday.

I didn't know at the time, as I do now, that Hodges' death would set the franchise back 10 years. I did know that losing Gil was going to create a huge void. The reason I knew that as an 18-year-old was that I had read what Tom Seaver and Bud Harrelson—idols of mine that were seemingly in awe of Hodges' abilities as a leader—were saying about him before he died. Also, just seeing how things got serious the minute he showed up, I just knew that Hodges loss was going to be a tough one from which to recover.

To take Hodges' place as manager—not a comfort zone for anyone— the Mets chose Yogi Berra. I had no problem with their choice—how can you ever object to Yogi for anything?—he was the logical man for the job. He was also the easiest for Mets fans to accept after losing an icon. Yogi was already in place with the Mets as one of their coaches and he was the only one of Hodges' coaches who had managed in the major leagues. He managed and won a pennant with the Yankees in '64, so I was fine with him as Hodges' replacement. What I didn't know then was that he wasn't the best guy for the job in the Mets organization.

No knock on Yogi, but the guy that should have gotten the job was Whitey Herzog, who was working for the Mets at the time. He had been their third-base coach one year under Westrum and then the Mets put him in charge of their minor leagues. Herzog was sharp, but he also was outspoken and opinionated. Had he remained with the Mets, he could have (and should have) eventually been their manager or general manager or both, but he couldn't get along with M. Donald Grant, the team's pompous chairman of the board. In short, Herzog had no respect for Grant's knowledge of baseball and made no secret of it.

In retrospect it was the combination of Hodges' death and Grant's disdain for Herzog that set the organization back those 10 years. Grant liked sycophants, and he also loved to rule officiously and exert his control by giving people a hard time. The only person in the organization that Grant could not intimidate was Gil Hodges, and once Gil died Grant had free rein.

To Berra's credit, the Mets got off to a sensational start in '72. They won 33 of their first 49 games, and on June 10 were in first place in the National League East, a game and a half ahead of the Pirates. But they would lose 57 of their last 107 games and finish in third place, 13½ games out.

In fairness to Berra, his team was hit with a rash of injuries in the second half. Nevertheless, there were rumblings that change was in the air and Berra's job was in jeopardy. It became clear that in order to save his job, he was under pressure to win in '73.

The Mets came flying out of the gate in '73, winning their first four games. They then proceeded to lose 13 of their next 21 to fall below .500 at 12–13. Berra's head was clearly on the chopping block. Things got so bad that the *New York Post* asked its readers to vote whether the Mets should fire chairman of the board Donald Grant, general manager Bob Scheffing, or Berra. Only the fact that the Mets had suffered an inordinate number of injuries to key players and that no team in the National League East was taking control of the division saved Yogi from being fired during the season.

On August 17, the Mets were in sixth place, 13 games under .500 at 53–66, but they were only 7½ games out of first, so I never stopped looking at the standings. But when a team is that many games under .500 that late in the season, you don't logically think about it making a run.

What turned the tide was that the injured began returning. Catcher Jerry Grote came back in July to help straighten out the pitching staff, and then when Buddy Harrelson returned on August 18 things really came together. His return glued the infield. Another factor was Tug McGraw, who had been horrible up to that point.

He'd lost six games and blown seven saves, but in the last five weeks he didn't lose a game or blow a save and he picked up four of his five wins and 12 of his 25 saves.

It was just about that time that the Mets adopted two slogans that would become rallying cries for the season and would also work their way permanently into the language both in and outside of baseball.

"You gotta believe," McGraw uttered one day, presumably as a spoof of M. Donald Grant after the chairman's attempt to motivate his floundering team with a Rockne-like postgame oratory. Soon, every Mets victory would elicit a rousing "You gotta believe" from McGraw and others.

"It ain't over 'til it's over," was the latest Yogi Berraism, declared by the manager after the Mets rallied from a huge deficit to win a game. Later, it would be used frequently to refer to the Mets comeback in the season. Eventually, it was adopted by athletes, coaches, politicians, and people from all walks of life to show their unwillingness to give in to defeat or failure.

All of a sudden you looked at the standings and the Mets were only a handful of games out of first and they had their team back together. Seaver was Seaver, Koosman had come around, Matlack, after a terrible start, was getting into a good groove, and McGraw was saving games again. The impossible no longer seemed impossible.

Starting on August 18, the Mets won 24 of their next 35 games. On September 21, they beat the Pirates 10–2 to even their record at 77–77 and move into first place, which they would not relinquish. They finished a game and a half ahead of the Cardinals with a record of 82–79 and a winning percentage of .509, the lowest in baseball history for a championship team.

Despite their record, there was optimism about the Mets' chances in the National League Championship Series. With a healthy Grote and Harrelson and their pitching Big Three and McGraw back on track, I knew that once they got into a short series the Mets could beat anybody. Even the Big Red Machine.

Chapter 7
A ROSE BY
ANY OTHER NAME

should hate Pete Rose because he tortured the Mets with a lifetime batting average against them of .302 for 335 games, 396 hits, 11 home runs, 109 runs batted in, 207 runs, and 136 walks, and because he almost separated the head of Bud Harrelson—one of my all-time favorite Mets—from his body one lovely 1973 Indian summer afternoon. Rose might be the No. 1 villain in Mets' history, or maybe No. 1A along with Chipper ("Larry, Larry") Jones.

Despite all that, I could never bring myself to hate Pete Rose. No way. He was a joy to watch, the embodiment of hustle, aggressiveness, competitiveness, hard work, overachievement, and desire. He just happened to wear the wrong uniform, but that wasn't his fault. Besides, how am I going to hate a guy named Rose?

My first encounter with Rose came when I was about 12 or 13 years old and it came in a non-professional situation. In the '60s, T-shirts that looked like football jerseys were all the rage for a couple of summers and I had one with red lettering and a large number 14 on the back, which I wore for Y.A. Tittle, at the time the All-Pro quarterback for the New York Giants. On top of the 14 I had my last name inscribed, so that the back of my jersey had "ROSE" on top and underneath it 14.

Quite by accident I happened to put on that T-shirt one day when a friend and I went to Shea Stadium for a game between the Mets and the Cincinnati Reds. Pete Rose, of course, wore No. 14 for the Reds. Before the game we were standing at the railing on the third-base side near the visitor's dugout and Rose was there holding court with the media. He spotted my T-shirt and said something like, "Hey, here's my New York fan." You can imagine how I felt like I was special because Pete Rose acknowledged me. This was around 1966 or '67, before he became a villain in New York, which would reach its crescendo that day in 1973.

I'm sorry to say that although our paths crossed from time to time, I never got to spend a great deal of time with Rose, who I have been told was a sportswriter's—and sportscaster's—dream because he had so much to offer and was so accommodating and interesting. Pete wouldn't know me from a hole in the wall, and he probably never knew my name because if he had he no doubt would have said something about the fact we have the same last name.

I did have a friend, a young woman who had been a college classmate of mine, who moved to Las Vegas after we graduated. I visited her once and she told me that she had neighbors, a mother and daughter, who said they were Pete Rose's best friends. This was in '78, the year Rose went on his 44-game hitting streak. That July, while the streak was ongoing, the Reds came to play the Mets at Shea Stadium, and after Pete had finished with the usual horde of reporters I was able to grab him at his locker for a few seconds and I mentioned this mother and daughter. He laughed and said, "Yeah, they're nice folks." I suspected he was trying to tell me they weren't as close friends as the mother and daughter implied they were, but he did acknowledge them and that was that. Other than that, I never had much contact with him except in group interviews when I was working for WCBS radio.

During the streak, Rose was the Pied Piper. When he came to Shea he was escorted up to the press level for interviews and there would be 70 to 80 members of the media following him in tow (today there would be five or 10 times that many). You could tell that Pete was loving all the attention. After one interview session, I hung in until the throng had drifted away and said to him, "You can't get away from this, can you?" I meant the swarm of reporters.

Pete just winked and said, "I can get away from it any time I want to." I interpreted that as tantamount to saying, "I don't want to get away from it."

Whatever emotions and admiration I had, or would eventually have, for Rose were irrelevant on the afternoon of October 8, 1973. On that day, Rose was only the enemy, part of a formidable opponent the Mets would have to beat to get to the World Series.

The Cincinnati Reds had won 99 games to win the National League West, 17 more than the Mets won to finish first in the East. They had Johnny Bench, Joe Morgan, and Tony Perez, each of whom had hit 25 home runs or more. Bench and Perez also both had more than 100 RBI. Rose led the league with a .338 average and 230 hits, and they had two other .300 hitters: Perez and Dan Driessen. The Mets had one hitter with more than 16 homers: John Milner with 23. Their RBI leader was Rusty Staub with 76, and their leading batter was Felix Millan at .290. In a dozen meetings between the two teams during the season, the Reds had won eight times.

But the Mets had their Big Three of Seaver, Koosman, and Matlack, with Tug McGraw in the bullpen.

The first two games of the best-of-five NLCS were played in Cincinnati, so I naturally figured the Mets needed to win one of those two games and they would have a great chance to reach the World Series. The Mets had Seaver and Matlack lined up to start those two games.

Seaver was brilliant in Game 1. He held the Reds to four hits through the first seven innings and would end up striking out 13. But the Mets could manage only three hits against Jack Billingham, one of those hits a double by Seaver in the second that scored Bud Harrelson, who had walked. And that's how it stood going into the bottom of the eighth, the Mets and Seaver up 1–0.

Then with one out in the eighth, Rose, who had hit only five home runs all year, hit one to tie the score 1–1. Bench homered in the ninth and the Mets, and Seaver, were beaten 2–1. It was a crushing defeat, especially because Seaver had been so dominant, but it was only one game and, as Yogi said, it ain't over 'til it's over.

As good as Seaver was in Game 1, Matlack was even better in Game 2. He held the mighty Big Red Machine to two hits—a pair of singles by veteran Andy Kosco—and struck out nine. The Mets scored a run in the fourth on a home run by Rusty Staub. The Mets went into the ninth inning leading 1–0, and then they broke the game open with four runs in the frame.

I was feeling pretty good after that game. The Mets had won the one game in Cincinnati that they needed and I was looking forward to Game 3 back in Shea Stadium the next day.

Monday, October 8, was a gorgeous day, a perfect fall baseball day. I was in my customary seat in the upper deck behind home plate and filled with anticipation and optimism as the Reds came to bat against Jerry Koosman in the top of the fifth inning. Rusty Staub had hit a home run with nobody on in the first and a home run with two runners on in the second. The Mets added a run in the third and two more in the fourth, so they were up 9–2 when Pete Rose stroked a one-out single to center. That brought up Joe Morgan.

I was thinking they have a big lead and they're at home, they're going to win this game and then try to win the pennant the next day and even if they lose that game they still have Seaver pitching in Game 5 at home. I watched Koosman get Morgan to hit a roller to first and I watched Milner field it cleanly, turn, and throw a strike to Harrelson at second.

I didn't see what happened next. Like most everyone else, I followed the play to first base because it was a double play and I saw Milner receive the return throw from Harrelson, but out of the corner of my eye I could see peripherally that there was a commotion going on around second base. I saw Rose and Harrelson rolling around on the ground but I was so intent on following the ball, I never did see Rose barrel into Harrelson at second and upend him until later on tape, after the fact.

After the scuffle had subsided—a typical baseball brawl, both benches emptying, a lot of pushing and shoving and very little fighting—and umpires had restored order, the game continued with the Mets coming to bat and the Reds taking the field in the bottom of the fifth. What I saw next made me sick to my stomach. Fans in and around the left-field seats began throwing all manner of garbage onto the field. Bottles, cans, fruit, just about anything they could get their hands on, they threw it onto left field because left field was where Rose was playing.

I kept thinking that this display of bad sportsmanship, this unruly, mob-like behavior, was so much different from '69. In '73, I was 19 years

Pete Rose and Bud Harrelson scuffle after Rose failed to break up a double play by going into Harrelson in Game 3 of the National League Championship Series on October 8, 1973. (AP Images)

old. I was 15 in '69. It was only a difference of four years, but it might as well have been 20 years. When the Mets clinched the pennant and then the World Series in '69 it was the year of Woodstock, and sure fans went on the field, but nobody was bent on destruction other than pulling up a little grass for a souvenir. In '73, I wasn't on the field when they clinched. I remember seeing the venom with which people came onto the field after Game 5. It was nothing like '69.

The last out in '73 was a ground ball to first base grabbed by John Milner, who flipped it to Tug McGraw covering first, and by the time McGraw stepped on the bag, he had 100 people surrounding him. The Mets had just won the pennant, but what was out there was an angry mob bent on destruction, which seemed to me to be a change in how fans were beginning to view sporting events.

I first witnessed that change during the New York Knicks' NBA championship season of 1969–70. I was sitting in the mezzanine for a game between the Knicks and Chicago Bulls and there was a call that went against the Knicks. Maybe because the Bulls were in town, somebody got the idea it would be cute to try this, and people started chanting "Bull----! Bull----! Bull----!"

I had never heard people say curse words in public. I would never be comfortable doing it. That was the start of it in my experience, and by '73 we had evolved to where whatever inhibitions people had about how they behaved in public and whatever decorum was expected was no longer in vogue. It was scary to me. I was sitting in the upper deck between home plate and third base and I remember the left-field area littered with garbage and Reds manager Sparky Anderson pulling his team off the field, which was not only his right but his duty to protect his players.

Then I followed as Yogi, Seaver, and Mays walked out to left field and pleaded with the fans to stop throwing bottles on the field because it was scary. It had a mob mentality. If it didn't stop, the game could have been forfeited to the Reds.

Having seen what it was like in '69, that when people are of a mind to do so, they can get out onto the field, I was afraid after the Rose-Harrelson incident that people were going to storm the field and create a full-scale riot. Since I was in the upper deck I knew I was protected from any harm, but that wasn't my main concern. I know there was a bigger issue at stake, but my concern was purely selfish. I was thinking, "Don't forfeit this game, you're ahead. Stop it! You're trying to win a pennant!"

Eventually order was restored. Neither Rose nor Harrelson was ejected from the game, which was a little surprising, and Koosman held the Reds to just two hits the rest of the way. The final score was 9–2, exactly as it was when the brawl erupted. Now the Mets were one win away from getting to the World Series.

To start Game 4, Berra chose veteran left-hander George Stone, who had come over with Felix Millan in a trade with the Braves that winter and who won 12 games and lost only three. He was brilliant for $6\frac{2}{3}$ innings, allowing just one run and three hits and leaving with the score tied 1–1. McGraw relieved him and, in a sign of the times, the Mets' "closer" would pitch $4\frac{1}{3}$ shutout innings, taking the game to the 12th inning.

With one out in the top of the 12th, here came trouble again. Rose hit a home run off Harry Parker and the Reds won 2–1 and evened the series. There would be a Game 5 in Shea Stadium on Wednesday afternoon, October 10, with Tom Seaver opposing Cincinnati's ace, Jack Billingham, each with identical regular season records of 19–10.

Seaver had the upper hand, pitching into the ninth inning, while the Mets drove Billingham out in a four-run fifth and coasted to a 7–2 victory and a date with the Oakland Athletics in the World Series.

The A's were the defending World Series champions, an American League 94-win powerhouse with three sluggers—Reggie Jackson, Sal Bando, and Gene Tenace—that combined for 85 home runs and 299 runs batted in, and a pitching staff that was more than the equal of the

Mets', with three 20-game winners—Catfish Hunter, Ken Holtzman, and Vida Blue—and a lockdown closer in Rollie Fingers.

Despite those impressive numbers, I was confident. If the Mets could beat the Big Red Machine, the Oakland Mustaches (they were the first team in the modern era to sport facial hair because their iconoclastic owner, Charles O. Finley, offered any of his players $300 to do so) should be no problem.

The surprising thing about the first four games (each team won two) was not that the A's out-pitched the Mets in Game 1 (Holtzman beat Matlack 2–1) and Game 3 (Hunter started against Seaver but neither was involved in the decision, a 3–2 win for Oakland), but that the Mets won Game 2 in a 10–7 shootout, and in the first four games the Mets, who hit 85 homers in the regular season to the A's 147, outscored their opponents 19–13 and out-homered them 4–0. When the Mets beat the A's 2–0 in Game 5 with Koosman pitching 6⅓ innings and McGraw 2⅔ innings (he would appear in five of the seven games and pitch 13⅔ innings after working in two games of the NLCS), the Mets were one win away from their second World Series championship, with two chances to get it in Oakland.

My confidence was based on the fact that the Mets were well fortified with pitching for those last two games with Seaver, Matlack, and Stone all available to pitch. By the same token, that availability of all three pitchers was forcing Berra to make a decision that would be discussed for years, is even still being discussed in some quarters today, and likely contributed to Yogi losing his job as manager of the Mets two years later.

I thought then, and still do to this day, that the right decision was to start Stone in Game 6 and then drop the big one, a fully rested Seaver, on them in Game 7. But Berra didn't consult me for my opinion, wouldn't have even if he knew me at the time, and wouldn't have let me sway him if he did know me and did consult me. His choice was to start Seaver in Game 6 and come back with Matlack, if needed, in Game 7.

I understood why Berra made the decision he did. He believed that when you have your opponents down, step on them; that Seaver and

Yogi Berra, Tug McGraw, and Willie Mays celebrate after winning Game 2 of the 1973 World Series. (Getty Images)

Matlack on three days' rest was a better option than Stone and Seaver on full rest; and he had more faith in Matlack, who had the hot hand with 23 innings, three runs, eight hits, and 17 strikeouts in three postseason starts, than he did in Stone.

I understood that there were many examples before and since in which great pitchers were both successful and unsuccessful pitching on short rest in big games.

And I also understood that Berra's decision, whatever it was, would be hailed if he won and condemned if he lost.

I held my ground, and still do. It was the wrong decision. There were stories over the years intimating that Seaver had gone to Yogi and demanded he pitch Game 6; that he wanted to close it out and Yogi said yes. Years later, I asked Seaver, not on the air and not for attribution, but privately, if that was true. And Tom said it was Yogi's call.

The operation was a success, but the patient died. Seaver pitched well enough to win: seven innings, six hits, two runs, both driven in on doubles by Reggie Jackson in the first and third. But Hunter pitched better: 7⅓ innings, four hits, one run. Trailing 2–0 in the eighth, Seaver left for a pinch-hitter, Ken Boswell, who singled to knock out Hunter. Left-hander Darold Knowles replaced Hunter and gave up singles to Wayne Garrett and Felix Millan.

Now it was 2–1, one out, and runners on first and third with Rusty Staub, the Mets' best hitter during that postseason, due up. Knowles struck out Staub on three pitches and Fingers came in to retire Cleon Jones on a fly ball. Fingers then closed out the 3–2 win and they went to a Game 7, Matlack against Holtzman.

Matlack failed to get out of the third inning when the A's took a 4–0 lead on a pair of two-run homers, the first by Bert Campaneris, the second by Jackson. When Jackson finished circling the bases he pounced on home plate with both feet in a flourish as if to punctuate the occasion. I was at home, watching on television, and when Reggie did that I wanted to put my foot through the screen. I doubt I was the only one. Holtzman pitched into the sixth and then the A's went to their bullpen—Knowles and Fingers—to finish off their second straight World Series title.

It was a bitter defeat for Mets fans. They had come so close against such overwhelming odds only to be denied a second World Series title. My disappointment at losing that seventh game lasted about a day. My overriding feeling, however, was that considering where the Mets came from, it was a great run. I was proud to know that there was going to be a pennant run up the pole in Shea Stadium on Opening Day of the following season, a new season bringing with it new hope.

Alas, it would be 13 years before the Mets would even get to the World Series again.

Chapter 8
SCOTT FREE

In my lifetime—and theirs—the Mets have won the World Series twice, in 1969 and 1986. Those two championships, as well as how I reacted to them, could not have been any more dissimilar.

In '69, I was a 15-year-old high school student, still a wide-eyed fan, filled with awe and wonder, hope and promise, still believing in miracles, and the Mets brought out all those emotions and fulfilled all my youthful hopes and dreams.

In '86, my life had a lot more definition and direction. I was an adult in '86, 32 years old, engaged to be married, and working as a professional sports reporter for WCBS radio, so my perspective for those two championship seasons was very different.

Also as different as night from day was how the two regular seasons unfolded. In '69, everything was a surprise and brand new, the Mets starting the season with very low expectations, coming from way back during the season, chasing and eventually catching the first-place Chicago Cubs, holding on and winning the World Series in one of the great upsets in baseball history.

In '86, the Mets blew it open so early that the pressure started to build in July. By July 4, they were 12½ games in front and winning the division was already a foregone conclusion. The pressure came from the idea that the Mets had better go all the way, and anything less than winning the World Series was going to scar that season. That's a tough burden to carry. The 1969 season was such a miracle and so unexpected that however passionate and loyal a fan I was at the age of 15, I never ever firmly believed that the Mets were going to win the World Series until Davey Johnson's fly ball nestled in Cleon Jones' glove for the final out.

In '86, I kept thinking they had to win. If they didn't win, it would be a disaster; the whole great season with everything they accomplished would be invalidated. And my perspective was different. In '69, I was just a fan and the players were all my heroes, bigger than life and rather remote. In '86, I was working and I had gotten to know some of those players. When you know the players involved, even though you try to maintain your objectivity and professionalism, you find yourself in your private moments rooting more for the people than for the team. Sure, I wanted the Mets to win, but I was focused more on certain individuals than on the whole. There were some guys associated with that team that I truly liked and cared about, and I wanted the Mets to win for their sake. For example, I had gotten to know Bud Harrelson fairly well and I wanted him to experience winning the World Series on two levels, as a player in '69 and as a coach in '86.

That '86 team acquired a reputation for being a bunch of rowdies and rollicking, battling cutups, hard to control and difficult to get along with, but I never found that to be true in my dealings with them. Even though I wasn't in the Mets employ in '86—I started working for them the following season—for some reason I had a great relationship with many of those players, even the so-called tougher ones like Keith Hernandez and Lenny Dykstra, both of whom had reputations for being tough to deal with. Dykstra was quirky and off-the-wall. He had a swagger and a demeanor that rubbed some people the wrong way, but I always got along well with him. He was cooperative with me, accessible and informative.

Doc Gooden was a lovable kid, easy to get along with. Darryl Strawberry was a little standoffish back then, but we eventually learned that he had been going through some issues in those days and in later years when he got his act together I found him to be easy to deal with and very intelligent.

I wasn't privy to what was going on behind the scenes in '86, so I never did see what was coming, but there were rumors. At first you thought it was just people out to shoot down the Mets because they were on top of the world. One of the rumors that surfaced was that Major League Baseball had information that some Mets were doing drugs. In fact, Ray Knight has said that someone high up in Major League Baseball told him, "You have prominent guys on this team that we think are involved in some stuff that if it doesn't stop there's going to be a real serious issue."

And of course it turned out to be true.

Whatever it was didn't come to light that season. Meanwhile, the Mets won 108 games, finished in first place in the National League East (by 21½ games), and faced the Houston Astros in one of the most exciting National League Championship Series ever, a best-of-seven series that started in Houston on Wednesday, October 8.

The theme of the series was established in that first game, when Houston's Mike Scott squared off against Dwight Gooden in a star matchup of pitchers who were the two most recent winners of the National League Cy Young Award.

Five weeks from his 22nd birthday, Gooden had blazed a trail in his first three major league seasons. He was a 17-game winner and NL Rookie of the Year in '84 and Cy Young Award winner in '85, with one of the greatest seasons any pitcher at any age ever recorded with a league-high 24 wins (against only four losses), an earned run average of 1.53, 16 complete games, 276.2 innings, and 268 strikeouts. While those totals dropped off slightly in 1986, he still won 17 games and struck out 200 batters.

Scott had been a promising second-round draft pick of the Mets in 1976, but after winning only 14 games in four seasons in New York, he was traded to Houston. While with the Astros, he had an encounter with

Roger Craig, guru of the split-finger fastball, himself a former Met. By '86, presumably because of the split-finger, he had become a star, an 18-game winner with a league-leading 2.22 ERA over 275.1 innings with 306 strikeouts. But there were rumors that his success was due to more than the split-finger, and reports of scuffed baseballs were widespread. How else could it be explained that a pitcher would jump from 137 strikeouts in '85 to 306 strikeouts a year later?

1969, 1973, 1986, 2000…so many great memories at Shea Stadium. Here I am with (left to right) Bud Harrelson, Tom Seaver, Darryl Strawberry, and Mike Piazza prior to the final weekend at Shea in 2008. (Photo: Marc S. Levine, New York Mets)

On September 25, Scott had pitched a no-hitter against the San Francisco Giants as the Astros clinched first place in the NL West. And now, 13 days later in Game 1 of the NLCS, he was almost as dominant against the Mets, holding them to five hits, all singles, and striking out 14 in a 1–0 victory. Gooden allowed only seven hits, but one of them was a home run in the second inning by Glenn Davis.

The Mets bounced back to win Game 2 by a score of 5–1, beating Nolan Ryan, still another former Met. Bob Ojeda masterfully scattered 10 hits to send the series back to New York tied at one game apiece.

Game 3 in Shea Stadium was a white-knuckler. The Astros scored two runs in the first and two in the second off Ron Darling, but then settled down for four scoreless innings. The Mets came back to tie it with four in the sixth, the big blow a three-run home run by Strawberry that sent the crowd into hysterics. The Astros scored an unearned run in the seventh and the Mets went to the ninth inning still down by a run. A defeat would leave them down two games to one with Mike Scott looming over the proceedings, ready to pitch Game 4 the next day.

Astros closer Dave Smith, third in the league with 33 saves, came in to pitch the bottom of the ninth and was promptly greeted by Wally Backman with a bunt single. A passed ball sent Backman, the tying run, to second. Pinch-hitter Danny Heep, who had been obtained from the Astros by the Mets in the trade for Scott, flied out to center field. That brought up Dykstra, called "Nails" by his teammates, as in "tough as…." On an 0–1 pitch, Nails, who had entered the game as a pinch-hitter in the seventh, lived up to his nickname by driving a pitch into the Mets' bullpen in right field as more than 55,000 fans went berserk. The Mets had forged ahead in the series, two games to one.

Following the game, in the interview room at Shea Stadium (which was actually the old New York Jets' locker room), Dykstra gave all of the assembled reporters a big laugh. He was asked when he had last hit a game-winning home run. His answer?

"When I played against my brother in Strat-O-Matic!"

Strat-O-Matic, of course, is the board game which creates cards for each Major League player based on a variety of statistics in an attempt to create a realistic reproduction of big-league games and seasons. Lenny didn't reveal which team he was "managing" and who had hit the game-winning homer, or how many years (or days) earlier it had been, but I am fairly certain that in the ensuing years, someone rolled the dice and a computer-generated Dykstra homered to win a game in the bottom of the ninth. Somehow, though, I don't think the celebration and euphoria matched what took place that Saturday afternoon at Shea.

As they feared, the Mets were stifled again in Game 4 by Scott, who was only slightly less effective than he had been in Game 1. He struck out only five batters and the Mets reached him for a run in the eighth inning, but by then the Astros were ahead 3–0. Scott closed it out to even the series at two games each.

Mike Scott, at this point, was clearly in the Mets' heads. They examined every ball that came back into their dugout, looking for, and often finding, scuff marks. Scott was not penalized, and the Mets were effectively "psyched out."

Game 5 was a game for the ages, a classic pitching matchup between 21-year-old Dwight Gooden and 39-year-old Nolan Ryan, Cy Young against Cy Old. The game didn't just live up to the hype, it exceeded it. Gooden tip-toed through the first four innings and held the Astros scoreless despite reaching Doc for four hits. Ryan was even better in his first four innings. In fact, he was perfect: 12 Mets up, 12 Mets down, seven by strikeout.

The Astros pushed across a run in the fifth and the Mets tied it in the bottom of the inning on the first hit off Ryan, a home run by Strawberry; a laser-beam tracer down the right-field line. From that point on, Ryan and Gooden threw nothing but goose eggs, Ryan leaving for a pinch-hitter in the 10th, having given up two hits and striking out 12, Gooden replaced by Jesse Orosco in the 11th.

They went to the bottom of the 12th tied 1–1, when with one out Backman reached on an infield single. Looking to get a big lead, Backman was caught off first on a pickoff attempt but reached second on a throwing error by pitcher Charlie Kerfeld. Keith Hernandez was purposely walked to fill the open base and bring up Gary Carter in a situation in which he would become familiar in the days ahead. Carter delivered a sharp single to center to score Backman with the winning run that sent the Mets back to Houston, one win away from the World Series.

Game 6 of the '86 NLCS has been called by many "the greatest baseball game ever played." I don't know about that, but if you judge the greatness of a game by the number of knots in one's stomach, I'd have to go along with that assessment. This was 16 innings, four hours and 42 minutes of angst with an entire season at stake. Although it was Game 6 of a best-of-seven championship series, because of the underlying theme of the series (meaning the spectre of Mike Scott), it was a Game 6 that had the feel of a Game 7.

I was able to go to the games in New York, but the games in Houston I watched on television in my apartment, alone, and to this day I don't know how anyone made it through that sixth game. It was such a roller-coaster ride of peaks and valleys, ups and downs.

The game was hardly a half-hour old when the Mets were in a 3–0 hole, the Astros having scored three times in the first inning off Bobby Ojeda. He would allow just one more hit through the fifth, but the Mets were still down 3–0 going to the ninth. At that point, things looked bleak. The Mets were doing nothing against Bob Knepper, who had allowed just two hits and struck out six through the first eight innings. As Bob Murphy used to say, he was wearing the Mets "on his watch chain."

The underlying theme was that if the Mets didn't win this Game 6, they would have to face Scott in Game 7 in Houston and by then the whole thing about Scott scuffing the baseball had taken on a life of its own. Going into the ninth inning of that game I had a lower feeling than in some of the worst years they had between 1977 and 1983.

And then in a flash, it all turned around. It began with a triple by Dykstra to start the ninth. Then a single by Mookie Wilson. Kevin Mitchell grounded out but Hernandez doubled to score Mookie and knock Knepper out of the game. Carter walked. Strawberry walked to load the bases. And Knight hit a sacrifice fly to right to score Hernandez. The score was tied; it was a new ballgame.

Roger McDowell came in to pitch the bottom of the ninth. He would be the unsung hero of the game for the Mets, pitching five innings and allowing only one hit in excruciating pressure. Over the years, it has become, at least to me, the most underrated pitching performance in Mets' history. People always remember McDowell as a hot-foot-giving jokester, but I always think first of his role in Game 6 of the 1986 NLCS.

In the top of the 14th, the Mets pushed across the go-ahead run with a single by Carter. Strawberry then walked, and Carter was thrown out at third on a sacrifice bunt attempt by Knight, but then a one-out single by Backman scored Strawberry.

Three outs away from the pennant, manager Davey Johnson called on Jesse Orosco to close it out, but Billy Hatcher tied the score with a one-out home run. Two outs away from the pennant, the usually reliable Orosco on the mound and the game was tied. I couldn't believe it. I was sitting in front of the television on my recliner and when Hatcher's ball left the park I just stood up and did a face-plant, collapsing with my face buried in my living room carpet. I distinctly remember thinking, "All right, it's just tied, get back up."

They went to the 16th inning. Strawberry doubled. Knight singled him home, going to second on the throw to the plate and to third on a wild pitch. Backman walked. Another wild pitch scored Knight and sent Backman to second. Orosco sacrificed Backman to third and Dykstra singled him home. The Mets led 7–4.

But the Astros were not done yet. With one out in the bottom of the 16th, Davey Lopes walked. Bill Doran singled him to second and he scored on Hatcher's single. It was 7–5 and the Astros had the tying runs on base. Dennis Walling forced Hatcher at second for the second out as Doran went to third and scored on a single by Davis. That brought up Kevin Bass, the Astros' second-leading home run hitter with 20. A home run or a long extra-base hit would give the Astros a come-from-behind win and shift the momentum in their favor with Scott available to pitch Game 7.

The count went to 3–2. Orosco wound up and delivered. Bass swung and missed. It was over. The Mets had avoided having to face Mike Scott for a third time. They had won the National League pennant and were going to the World Series for only the third time in their history, the first time in 13 years.

Chapter 9
BUCKNER'S BOOT

Mets fans who believed they had reached the zenith of anxiety—and experienced the mother lode of joy—with Game 6 of the 1986 National League Championship Series in Houston, soon discovered they were mistaken. They hadn't seen anything yet, which we were to learn just 10 days later in New York, in the World Series against the Boston Red Sox, again in a Game 6.

Having come through the heart-palpitating, six-game series against the Astros, we settled down to what we thought would be a nice old-fashioned, enjoyable seven-game World Series against the Boston Red Sox. Wrong again!

If their fans thought the Mets, who hadn't won the World Series in 17 years and hadn't been in one in 13 years, were long-suffering, think how deprived were fans of the Red Sox, who had gone 68 years since winning the World Series. Their woes went all the way back to 1918, when a 23-year-old left-handed pitcher named George Herman Ruth, nicknamed "Babe," won two games against the Chicago Cubs to help the Red Sox win the Series for the third time in four years. Two years later, Ruth was sold to the New York Yankees for $125,000 in what would come to be known in Boston as "The Curse of the Bambino."

The '86 Red Sox were a powerful array of stars led by American League–batting champion Wade Boggs (.357), Jim Rice (.324, 20 homers, 110 RBI), and 24-game-winner Roger Clemens. The Sox won 95 games and finished five and a half games ahead of the Yankees in the American League East. They'd also just come through a heart-pounding, seven-game series of their own against the California Angels.

At the time I was working for WCBS radio, an all-news station doing sports updates at various times of the day, often on weekends. Our station's budget didn't allow for us to travel to away games during the postseason and because we were all news and had half a dozen sports reporters, we were granted only one credential per game at home, which we had to share among us. For games I was assigned to cover, I got our station's one seat in the auxiliary press box that was set up along the right-field line. For the games I was not assigned to cover, I managed to purchase tickets for seats in the upper deck behind home plate, for years my usual location.

As it turned out, I was assigned to work the famous (or infamous, depending on your point of view and rooting interest) Game 6 at Shea Stadium with the Mets' season on the line. They trailed in the Series, three games to two, so a loss would end their season in bitter disappointment.

But I'm getting ahead of myself. The Series opened in New York on Saturday night, October 18, just three days after the Mets' incredible, 16-inning win in Houston. Ron Darling started for the Mets against left-hander Bruce Hurst in what would be a pitching classic. Darling pitched seven innings, allowed three hits, and struck out eight, but left trailing 1–0, the Red Sox having scored an unearned run in the seventh on an error by Mets second baseman Tim Teufel.

Hurst pitched eight innings and also struck out eight. His victory was saved by Calvin Schiraldi, a former Met who had been sent to the Red Sox the previous November in a trade that brought Bobby Ojeda to New York. Mets manager Davey Johnson was not a big fan of Schiraldi's, and felt the Mets would eventually "get him" at a crucial juncture of a game. Stay tuned.

The Red Sox jumped all over Doc Gooden in Game 2, scoring three runs in the third, one in the fourth, and two in the fifth. Gooden gave up eight hits, including home runs by Dwight Evans and Dave Henderson, and the Sox rolled to a 9–3 victory.

Gone was the Mets' so-called home-field advantage, as historians pointed out that only one team in baseball history had ever come back to win the World Series after losing the first two games at home (and that took place just the previous season when the Royals came back to beat the Cardinals in seven games). With the next three games scheduled for Boston's ancient and historic (it was built in 1912) Fenway Park, the Mets' most fervent hope was to get the Series back to New York.

Monday, October 20, was a travel day, with Game 3 scheduled for Tuesday night, October 21. It is customary for the visiting team to stage a practice on the travel day in order to become acquainted with the nuances of playing in an unfamiliar ballpark. But Mets manager Davey Johnson, ever the psychologist and always unconventional, chose to eschew the practice, deciding that what his team needed more than practice was to get away from baseball for a day and clear their heads.

The strategy worked to perfection as the Mets came out swinging against Dennis "Oil Can" Boyd, with their first four hitters hitting safely and scoring. They would pound Boyd for six runs and nine hits in seven innings while Ojeda bewitched his former team with one run and five hits over seven innings in a 7–1 victory.

Game 4 produced more of the same for the Mets, a 6–2 victory with Lenny Dykstra hitting a home run for the second straight day, Gary Carter hitting two and driving in three runs, and Darling pitching seven scoreless, four-hit innings. Now the Series was tied. Until, that is, Hurst went into his magic act again in Game 5, pitching out of one jam after another and beating the Mets 4–2 despite giving up 10 hits.

The Mets pointed out that they had achieved their goal of bringing the World Series back to New York, but made no mention of the fact that

A great thrill for me was getting to emcee the 20th anniversary reunion of the 1986 world champion Mets. (Photo: Marc S. Levine, New York Mets)

they had to win those last two games at home to avoid the season ending in disaster.

I was assigned by WCBS radio to cover Game 6 of the World Series on the night of Saturday, October 25, an assignment I was going to have to handle with decidedly mixed emotions. On one hand I was filled with anxiety and dread for this game that could end, and define, the Mets season. On the other hand, I was being paid to be an objective reporter and to provide information that was not tinged with any preference, bias, or rooting interest.

As the game unfolded, the Red Sox put up single runs off Bobby Ojeda in the first and second innings and took their 2–0 lead into the fifth with their ace, Roger Clemens, blazing, having held the Mets hitless and striking out six.

However, Darryl Strawberry walked to open the bottom of the fifth and promptly stole second (Darryl's career is marked by his enormous power that produced so many tape-measure home runs but not enough is made of his speed and base-running ability). Ray Knight singled Strawberry home and Mookie Wilson followed with a single to right. When the ball was bobbled by Dwight Evans, Knight raced around to third. Danny Heep, pinch-hitting for Rafael Santana, rapped into a double play, but Knight scored on the play, an unearned run that tied the score at 2–2.

After giving up two runs, Ojeda settled down, held the Sox scoreless through the sixth, and was replaced by Roger McDowell, who started the seventh by walking Marty Barrett. Barrett took second when Bill Buckner followed by grounding out to the right side. Jim Rice then reached base when third baseman Ray Knight bobbled his ground ball, putting runners on first and third. McDowell got Evans to ground to second, a potential inning-ending double-play ball, but Rice was safe at second and Barrett scored an unearned run that gave Boston a 3–2 lead.

Rich Gedman followed with a sharp single to left that was fielded by Mookie Wilson, who came up throwing and nailed Rice at the plate. We didn't know it at the time, but not only would the throw be a game-saver, it wouldn't even be Wilson's greatest heroic moment of the game.

Clemens retired the Mets in order in the bottom of the seventh, but when the Mets came to bat in the eighth, Red Sox manager John McNamara had changed pitchers. He removed his ace Clemens, who allegedly told the manager he was out of gas after allowing two runs (one earned), four hits, and striking out eight, and replaced him with Calvin Schiraldi, who yielded the tying run on a sacrifice fly by Gary Carter.

The score stood at 3–3, and when the Red Sox failed to score against Rick Aguilera in the top of the ninth and the Mets failed to score against Schiraldi in the bottom of the inning, the game went to the 10th inning—nail-biting time.

Dave Henderson led off the top of the 10th with a home run and you could feel the hope seep out of the capacity Shea Stadium crowd like air oozing out of a balloon. To exacerbate the mood of depression and resignation, the Red Sox tacked on another run on a two-out double by Boggs and an RBI single by Barrett.

A two-run lead seemed insurmountable, even against Schiraldi. I had pretty much resigned myself to the disappointment of another close-but-no-cigar season gone awry and reminded myself to suppress my dejection because I had a job to do. My assignment, in part, was upon the final out of the game, to record a quick 30-second "voicer" that included all the salient facts, the final score, the Red Sox clinching their first World Series in 68 years, the winning pitcher, the star of the game, etc., and then run downstairs to the clubhouses and get interview material.

I was in my seat in the auxiliary press box down the right-field line, suffering as I watched the Red Sox build their two-run lead. The way we did it on WCBS radio, I was to call into the news room at the start of the final half inning and say, "Just roll tape and monitor it. I'll let you know when there's one out, two out, and when the final out is made, I'll record my 30-second piece and head downstairs. But be sure to monitor the tape so you know when I'm finished."

The tape started to roll and I was sitting there watching the whole season go down the tubes as Wally Backman led off the bottom of the 10th with a fly ball to left. I said into the tape, "One out." Keith Hernandez came next and flied out to center field, and I said, "Two out."

Two out, nobody on base, the Mets down to their final out, and Gary Carter coming to bat. Years later we were to learn that after he made the second out, Hernandez, a fierce competitor, was so dejected that he left the dugout and went into the Mets clubhouse and sat in the manager's office smoking a cigarette and drinking a beer. We also learned that as he stepped in the batter's box, Carter kept telling himself, "You're not going to be a trivia question sometime in the future. You're not going to make the final out of the World Series."

Carter looped a single to left and I droned, "There's a base hit."

Next up was Kevin Mitchell, pinch-hitting for Rick Aguilera. He lined a single to center. "Oh," I said, a little more animated now, "there's another base hit."

When Ray Knight followed with a hit to center that scored Carter, I really got excited, my voice rising a few decibels, "Here's another base hit, the tying run's at third…."

Schiraldi was replaced by Bob Stanley and the crowd that had been sitting in stunned silence just moments earlier was going wild. And then Stanley threw a wild pitch that scored Mitchell, tying the game 5–5 and sending Knight to second with the winning run. And finally, of course, there was the ground ball by Mookie Wilson that trickled through Bill Buckner's legs at first base and into right field as Knight rounded third and scored the winning run. I was yelling into the telephone, "I don't believe it! Knight scores! The Mets win! This is one of the most unbelievable things I've ever seen!" Screaming at the top of my lungs because I knew none of this was going on the air. I'm sorry to say that everything I said into the tape in the bottom of the 10th inning of that game was erased, which is a shame, because I would have liked to have had it as a keepsake. That was my fault and I kick myself for not telling them to save the tape, because I would have had a great piece of memorabilia. What I do have are memories of that unbelievable night.

In retrospect, there were two things that came out of those frenetic final moments of the sixth game. One was a story that sometime in the bottom of the 10th, a technician inadvertently hit a button that activated on Shea Stadium's huge message board in left-center field a statement congratulating the Boston Red Sox on winning the 1986 World Series. I'm not suggesting that the story of the premature message is an urban legend, but I didn't see the message, and I don't know anybody who did.

The other story has to do with the ill-fated Bill Buckner, who was a 36-year-old, 17-year major league veteran at the time that he became the unfortunate goat of that World Series. Buckner had been hobbled with a leg injury and, in fact, in the Red Sox's three victories, manager John McNamara had removed Buckner from the game for defense in the late innings and replaced him with Dave Stapleton. But in Game 6, McNamara failed to replace Buckner and later explained that he wanted to acknowledge Buckner's distinguished career (he would play 22 major league seasons and finish with 2,715 hits and 1,208 RBI) and to experience the honor of being on the field, to share in the celebration when the Red Sox, at long last, had finally clinched a World Series victory.

One other note from the aftermath of Game 6: in the interview room I asked Mookie if the enormity of what just happened had started to sink in. At least, that's what I was trying to convey. Instead, I asked in a voice and tone filled with incredulity, which was certainly the emotion of the hour, "Do you realize what just happened here?" For some reason, everyone in the room burst out laughing, and some with personal connections to the Mets (family and friends) who were in the room at the time, started to cheer. Believe me, I had not been looking for applause, but given the moment, the simplicity of the question along with it's inflection, combined, in retrospect, to become one of my favorite questions I've ever posed in an interview.

Mookie had an almost dazed, even wistful, expression as he simply answered, "I'm really not sure, but I know we're playing tomorrow!" More cheers, although, of course, not from the press.

That reaction, and Mookie's as well, confirmed that we had all just witnessed something for the ages. I had never heard cheering in an interview room before; and I haven't since. In fact, I'm not sure that I ever will again. One thing has been made abundantly clear over the years, however. The legacy and long-term significance of moments like that depend in large part on what follows. For the Mets, as well as the Red Sox, there was still one more game to play.

Game 7 was, for several reasons, anticlimactic. Scheduled for Sunday, October 26, the game was postponed because of rain and played on Monday, October 27. I was not assigned to work so I was able to attend the game simply as a fan, sit in my usual seat, and cheer the Mets to my heart's content. Although the score was tied 3–3 after six innings, just as it was after eight innings in Game 6, the seventh game couldn't measure up to the drama and intensity of Game 6. Nothing could.

The Mets broke the tie with three runs in the seventh against Schiraldi, making a prophet of Davey Johnson, and the Sox came back with two in the eighth to make it 6–5. But when the Mets scored two in the bottom of the eighth, and had Jesse Orosco on the mound in the ninth, Shea breathed easier. When Orosco retired the first two batters in the top of the ninth, nobody believed the Red Sox could do in the ninth inning of Game 7 what the Mets had done in the 10th inning of Game 6. And they didn't. Orosco struck out Marty Barrett, and the Mets were world champions for the second time in their history.

Looking back on that ninth inning in '86, I feel I demonstrated a concession to maturity and professionalism, as well as remarkable restraint and self-control, by not giving in to the temptation of charging onto the field for a souvenir as I had done in '69. Police on horseback made sure that nobody else did, either.

Chapter 10
THE "LOAN" RANGER

From the moment I stumbled quite by accident upon a Rangers hockey game on my transistor radio and heard Marv Albert for the first time, I dreamed of following in the footsteps of my childhood hero. Nearly a quarter of a century later my dream came true. I was following my idol, but not in his footsteps. It was January 1985, and here I was in Madison Square Garden, sitting for the first time in the seat Marv had occupied for so many years and broadcasting a Rangers game on radio. It was, and still is, the biggest thrill of my professional career.

Marv's schedule was escalating. He was doing Rangers and Knicks games and NBC was beginning to use him more and more on network coverage, all of which resulted in conflicts in his schedule. A replacement for him was needed. At the time I was working freelance and was available. Once again, I became indebted to Marv for recommending me as his fill-in and enabling me to fulfill my boyhood dream, even if only occasionally.

It was a bit of a risk for Marv to recommend me as his fill-in because I had no professional play-by-play background, except for one year when I did indoor soccer. It was a hard sell for him to get the people at the MSG network to give me a shot. They were reluctant to take that leap of faith, but Marv, bless him, persisted. He kept plugging away, saying, "Give him a chance," and eventually, the powers-that-be relented.

The 1994 Rangers broadcast team: Sal Messina, Marv Albert, and me.
(Photo: George Kalinsky)

For a few years, I filled in for Marv very occasionally, but as his responsibilities with NBC grew, he became less and less available to do Rangers hockey. Finally, in '89, MSG recognized the need for a permanent replacement for Marv and they hired me to fill that role, again at Marv's urging. By then, even though Marv was still the primary voice of Rangers hockey and I was technically his backup, because of his other commitments I was doing more games than he was.

That was the situation for seven years. It was a period in which I was able not only to gain valuable play-by-play experience but to feed my passion for the game of hockey. During that time I had some unbelievable experiences, not the least of which was the 1993–94 season. That was an Olympic year, and John Davidson, who was the television color analyst on Rangers games, was hired by CBS as its ice hockey expert. So off he went to Lillehammer, Norway, for a few weeks, setting off a chain reaction in the Rangers' coverage. Sal Messina, who was my partner/ analyst on radio, replaced JD on television, and that left open the radio analyst's position. To fill the gap it was decided that they would bring in a rotating series of different color analysts, hockey experts with a Rangers background, among them their former goaltender, coach, and GM Emile "the Cat" Francis.

Sharing the microphone with Francis was a particular thrill for me. I fell in love with the Rangers and Emile Francis when I was 12 years old. That was my entry into hockey. I had met Emile briefly years earlier, but we really didn't know each other. For the benefit of the broadcast I thought it would be a good idea for the two of us to get together so we could become familiar and establish some sort of on-air rapport.

Our first game working together was going to be in Quebec and we had arranged to meet for lunch in the hotel on the afternoon of the game. It happened to be the weekend I turned 40 years old, so I looked upon this meeting with one of my early sports heroes as sort of a birthday present to myself. All the way down the elevator and into the restaurant on my way to meet up with Francis, I kept telling myself, "Now don't be a little wide-eyed hero worshipper. Make believe you're an experienced, sophisticated professional who is used to meeting boyhood favorites. Don't sit down and say, 'Hey, remember when you made this trade? Remember this game and that game?'"

I walked into the restaurant and there was Emile waiting for me.

"Emile, I'm Howie. How are you doing?"

The hostess showed us to a table and we sat down. My butt wasn't even warm when Francis said, "Have I ever told you about the time I made the deal so we could get the draft choice that I used to get Steve Vickers?"

It was one story after another and I was in my glory. It was a gift! It was as if I had won in a raffle a two-hour personal lunch with Emile Francis in which he would talk about everything I remembered about the Rangers since I was a kid and fell head over heels in love with hockey. Doing a few games on the air with him as my color analyst was a treat beyond my wildest dreams. He was fantastic. He had total recall and a sense of humor that was beyond belief. He regaled me, and our audience, with one story after another, embracing every story because that's his legacy.

A few months later, I had the great fortune of being on the air to experience another dream come true as the Rangers—the team I loved since I was a kid—were in the midst of a run to the Stanley Cup championship. At the same time, because of my long history as a Rangers fan and the emotion involved, I was embarking on the hardest few weeks of broadcasting I've ever done.

Two separate agendas were set to clash, and I had to make sure not to allow that to happen. First was the huge fan in me, which caused me, during the playing of the national anthem before every game, to turn and look up at the old seats I occupied as a former season-ticket holder. I did that intentionally to remind myself how lucky I was to be down in the broadcast booth. But as passionate as I was as a fan, and as emotional as this experience was, I had to keep that all in check while I was doing the game. Certainly the natural attitudes, emotions, and passions you have enter into a broadcast, but on the other hand they can't be the overriding element. You have to be professional. You have to be objective. You have to be on the play without coloring it or tailoring it in any way. As a result, my stomach was in knots during the entire playoffs, not just over whether the Rangers were going to win or lose but more because of that unbelievably palpable tug of war that was going on inside of me. I literally felt my stomach being pulled apart from trying to balance the passion against the professionalism.

Eventually, it gets easier. The deeper into your career you get the more natural it is to reconcile your fandom with your professionalism, because in a parallel sense, as your career evolves so does your personal life. You're no longer a 15-year-old kid sitting at home forgetting about school and homework and everything to go full-bore into rooting for the Mets or the Rangers. As you get older and you have a family and responsibilities, just as the realities of life take hold, they also take precedence. So your fanaticism finds its way—or at least it should. And I believe it did for me.

As the Rangers closed in on the '94 Stanley Cup—they blitzed the New York Islanders in a four-game sweep in the Eastern Conference Quarterfinals, overpowered the Washington Capitals four games to one in the Conference Semifinals and squeezed past the New Jersey Devils in a seven-game, nail-biting, heart-thumping Eastern Conference Finals— Marv Albert was able to get a special waiver from NBC to leave the NBA Finals on off-days and broadcast Games 5 and 7 of the Stanley Cup Finals between the Rangers, and the Vancouver Canucks. Both those games were potential clinchers for the Rangers, and after all his years broadcasting Rangers games it was only fitting that Marv be on the air when (if) the Rangers finally won the Cup.

Since I had done the bulk of Rangers games that season, Marv insisted that I do play-by-play in the second period of both Games 5 and 7. It was a thoughtful gesture on his part and something he obviously didn't have to do. He certainly could have done the entire game. After all, he's Marv Albert. He wrote the book on radio play-by-play of Rangers hockey. On radio, in fact, he *was* New York Rangers hockey. But he graciously chose to step aside and allow me to have a part of history, and I will never forget his kindness and consideration.

Here I am kissing the 1994 Stanley Cup, won by the team of my youth—the New York Rangers.

Leading three games to one, the Rangers sought to close out the series in Game 5 in front of a deliriously wild and eager Madison Square Garden crowd, but it was not to be, as the Canucks stayed alive with a 6–3 victory and brought the series back to Vancouver for Game 6. There, the Canucks took a 4–1 victory to set up a winner-take-all, sudden-death Game 7 back at the Garden.

The seventh game was pure torture. The Rangers were able to take a 3–1 lead on Mark Messier's goal midway through the second period and then, after the Canucks hit two posts and came close to tying the game a couple other times, hold on for a 3–2 victory to capture their first Stanley Cup in 54 years; in other words, the first in my lifetime.

Marv had the call as the final seconds ticked off, as he should have, and while I had the satisfaction of calling part of the championship game, I wasn't the one who said "...and the Rangers win the Stanley Cup!" That was Marv. I still have not experienced the complete euphoria of being on the air and proclaiming my team as Stanley Cup or World Series champions.

Maybe I'll have that opportunity soon.

One can only hope. In the meantime, I was fortunate enough to make a call during the Rangers' run to the Cup that seems to have taken on a life of its own.

Chapter 11

MATTEAU! MATTEAU! MATTEAU!

I have broadcast more than 2,500 New York Mets games and more than 1,300 New York Islanders games without having had the thrill and satisfaction of describing a World Series championship or a Stanley Cup title. But in fewer than 500 New York Rangers games, I not only called a portion of a Stanley Cup championship, I received more attention and recognition for a call I made than for anything I ever said over the airwaves with the Mets and Islanders; a call of just three words… or more precisely, one word.

I am flattered and extremely grateful that this call has popped up on several lists of "The Most Memorable Calls by Sportscasters." I'm also somewhat overwhelmed and surprised by the attention, because at the time I thought I had blown the call.

To set the scene, this was Game 7 of the Eastern Conference Finals in the 1994 Stanley Cup playoffs, the Rangers against the New Jersey Devils in Madison Square Garden on May 27, 1994. Stephane Matteau had won Game 3 with a double-overtime goal that put the Rangers up two games to one. Now, in the climactic Game 7, the Rangers and Devils again went into heart-pounding, nail-biting overtime, where one mistake

111

could send one team to the Stanley Cup Finals and end the season for the other.

There was a similarity between this game and Bobby Thomson's game-winning, pennant-winning home run off Ralph Branca in the 1951 National League playoff. I'm not suggesting that my call of Stephane Matteau's winning goal at 4:24 of the second overtime period is in a class with Russ Hodges' call of Thomson's home run, but there is a similarity in the two events in that whoever won the game between the Giants and Dodgers in 1951 was going to the World Series and whoever won this game in Madison Square Garden 43 years later was going to the Stanley Cup Finals. Both moments were climactic and packed with more emotion than often seems possible in sports. Both games also featured two teams from the same city or market. Two bitter rivals.

Here was my call as it has been preserved through the years:

Fetisov for the Devils plays it cross-ice into the far corner. Matteau swoops in to intercept. Matteau behind the net, swings it in front…he scores! Matteau! Matteau! Matteau! Stephane Matteau! And the Rangers have one more hill to climb, baby! But it's Mount Vancouver! The Rangers are headed to the Finals!

The call was spontaneous; I obviously couldn't have scripted it. But I will confess that as the game wound down with the Rangers leading 1–0, I was thinking to myself, "All I want to do when this game is over is just say something simple and let the crowd carry it for a couple of seconds." It was radio, and on radio you can't let the crowd go too long; you have to start filling in the blanks. I had planned that when the final buzzer rang I would say, "Now there's one more hill to climb." And then let the crowd carry it for a couple of seconds.

How could I know that the Devils would tie the score with seven seconds remaining in regulation? That they would go into a second overtime? That Matteau would score the winning goal?

I certainly didn't say to myself that whoever scores the winning goal I will say his name three times and speak almost indecipherably, but as I

was screaming Matteau's name that whole "one more hill to climb" thing popped into my head and for some reason, because they would be playing the Vancouver Canucks for the Stanley Cup, I threw in Mount Vancouver.

The deed was done, and then came the doubts. My first concern was that I had the wrong guy scoring the goal, a sportscaster's greatest fear; it was conceivable Esa Tikkanen might have gotten his stick on the puck, but looking carefully at the replay during the postgame show I was relieved to see that wasn't the case. It was clearly Matteau's goal.

The postgame show was the first time I heard myself on the call and listening to it brought me down. My heart sank. I found myself regretting making the call. I had never heard myself out of control like that and I thought, "Oh, no. This is a little bit much." Leaving the Garden I was really down, but when I walked out of the building and was headed for the parking lot across the street, there was a guy sitting in his car at the curb and he recognized me and said, "Hey, Howie, great call, great call." I thought he was just an excited Rangers fan because they won and this was a euphoric moment for him. I figured I wouldn't get nearly such a reaction from Devils fans. In fact, the current Islanders director of communications, Kimber Auerbach, was a big Devils' fan who grew up in New Jersey, and to this day he tells me, "I hated that call. I was haunted by that call." I certainly understand his reaction. After all, what does a Dodger fan think of Russ Hodges' call of Bobby Thomson's home run?

On my drive home I had WFAN on the car radio and the host, Steve Somers, and even the listeners calling in, were spending as much time talking about the call as they did about the game. They kept playing the call over and over and over and the people calling in were saying things like, "Oh my God, I got goose bumps."

The next day I drove to Shea Stadium for a day game and Russ Salzburg was hosting a show on WFAN, and the same thing happened. They were talking more about the call than about the game, and that baffled me. I couldn't understand why, when the Rangers had just won one of the great games in the history of the sport, they were talking about the call. That's when I began thinking that this thing was taking on a life of its own, and I no longer regretted making the call or being "out of control."

The bottom line is it has had legs and I'm very appreciative of that, especially when it's mentioned among some of the legendary calls by sportscasters through the years.

I'm not only a sportscaster, I'm also a radio/TV junkie. As such, here in no particular order are some of (in my opinion) the greatest calls ever by sportscasters. I hasten to point out that, for the most part, memorable calls by sportscasters are usually brought about by memorable events:

Stephane Matteau moments before he puts the puck past Martin Brodeur in double overtime to give the Rangers a 3–2 Game 3 win. (AP Images)

• Russ Hodges and "The Shot Heard 'Round the World."

There's a long drive…It's gonna be, I believe…the Giants win the pennant! The Giants win the pennant! The Giants win the pennant! The Giants win the pennant! Bobby Thomson hits into the lower deck of the left-field stands! The Giants win the pennant and they're goin' crazy! They're goin' crazy! Heeeey-oh!

That's the granddaddy of all great calls by a sportscaster and, in my opinion, No.1 on my list. I still get goose bumps every time I hear it, and I wasn't even born when he said it.

• Al Michaels' brilliant call as the clock ticked down in the U.S. hockey team's 4–3 victory over a heavily-favored Russian squad in the 1980 Olympics at Lake Placid.

Do you believe in miracles? Yes!

• Howard Cosell's call of George Foreman's 1973 KO of Joe Frazier.

Down goes Frazier! Down goes Frazier! Down goes Frazier!

• Vin Scully, with his call of Sandy Koufax's 1965 perfect game against the Cubs.

It is 9:46 PM. Two and two to Harvey Kuenn, one strike away. Sandy into his windup, here's the pitch. Swung on and missed, a perfect game.

On the scoreboard in right field it is 9:46 PM in the city of Angels, Los Angeles, California. And a crowd of 29,139 just sitting in to see the only pitcher in baseball history to hurl four no-hit, no-run games. He has done it four straight years, and now he caps it: on his fourth no-hitter he made it a perfect game.

The way Scully kept stating the time and marking the game for posterity was the most brilliant storytelling I have ever heard by a sportscaster on the radio. Scully said he did that as a favor to Koufax, who he figured would like to have the tape for his grandkids to hear some day.

• Jack Buck's call of Kirby Puckett's game-winning home run for the Minnesota Twins against the Atlanta Braves in the 11th inning of the sixth game of the 1991 World Series.

…and we'll see you tomorrow night.

I include this because exactly 20 years and one day later, in the 2011 World Series between the St. Louis Cardinals and the Texas Rangers, also in the 11th inning of the sixth game, this is how the late Jack Buck's son, Joe, called David Freese's game-winning home run for the Cardinals.

Freese hits it in the air to center…we will see you tomorrow night.

I got tears in my eyes when I heard that, because he just had the chance to tie in his father's words in an identical situation, and he had the presence of mind to do it. What a feeling that must have been for Joe.

• Clem McCarthy in 1938 describing Joe Louis' one-round knockout of Max Schmeling in Yankee Stadium.

Louis missed with a left swing but in close-quarters brought over a hard one to the jaw and again a right to the body, a left hook, a right to the head, a left to the head, a right. Schmeling is going down. But he held to his feet, held to the ropes, looked to his corner in helplessness. And Schmeling is down. The count is four. And he's up and Louis, right and left to the head, and Donovan is watching carefully. Louis measured him, right to the body, a left to the jaw. The count is five. Five, six, seven, eight, the men are in the ring. The fight is over. On a technical knockout. Max Schmeling is beaten in one round.

McCarthy's gravelly voice and frantic delivery made this call special.

• Jack Buck's radio call of an injury-hobbled Kirk Gibson's pinch-hit, game-winning, two-run home run off Dennis Eckersley for the Dodgers' 5–4 victory over the Athletics in Game 1 of the 1988 World Series.

I don't believe what I just saw.

• Vin Scully's call on the same play:

High fly ball into right field. And she is…gone. (Long pause under crowd noise) *In a year that has been so improbable, the impossible has happened.*

The brilliance of Scully's call wasn't the home run, it's what he said afterward. That's what television does; it allows you to say something profound, but generally speaking, after the fact. It's not as fulfilling as radio.

When you watch a game on television, the connection you make as a viewer is between your eyes and the event, the team, or a particular player, whoever it is that has done something extraordinary.

On radio, the connection you make is with the guy delivering the information. It's a tremendous responsibility to paint that word picture, to take a blank canvas and create a vivid, dynamic word image. That's what makes radio calls so special. That's why I love radio.

I learned a great deal from Gary Cohen in the few years I sat with him in the Mets' radio booth. Gary is such a sound tactician, and one thing I picked up from him is that when you're doing radio, the call doesn't end when the play is over. You have to describe the scene after the play.

One of the calls I'm most proud of came at Yankee Stadium on June 12, 2009. It was the Mets' first game at the new Yankee Stadium and I was on the radio. It was the bottom of the ninth inning, the Mets were ahead 8–7, there were two outs and runners on first and second, the tying run, Derek Jeter, on second, the winning run, Mark Teixiera, on first, and Alex Rodriguez at bat against Frankie Rodriguez. On a 3–1 pitch, ARod hit an easy fly ball to shallow right field that had a little hang time and I was getting ready to go into my usual close when the Mets record the final out for a victory: Put it in the books. But then Luis Castillo, the Mets' second baseman, dropped the ball, this easiest of pop-flies that even a Little Leaguer could catch. This is what I said:

Jeter comes around to score…here comes Teixiera digging for the plate… he slides in ahead of the throw…and the Yankees win the game.…

I liked that call a lot because I thought it was properly descriptive, properly emotional. It was such a shocking moment. I lean on emotion over detail. I'll take a little bit of emotion at the expense of a little bit of detail as long as the announcer doesn't eschew the basics. I've been at this business long enough that by now I'm trained to be detailed. My orientation at that point was to be purely reportorial because what was happening was almost unfathomable. I'm getting ready to say, "Put it in the books," and in fact I probably had the "P" on my lips, and instead, my voice laced with incredulity, I said, "He dropped the ball."

I had to edit myself there because my first reaction was, "He dropped the [bleeping] ball." But you're trained to go into whatever mode it is that triggers responsibility and my responsibility, at that moment was to describe what was happening on the field.

But my call that night didn't end when the Yankees scored the winning run. I couldn't just say, "...and the Yankees win the game." My function was to describe the scene, the Yankees mobbing ARod, who did nothing but hit an easy infield pop-up, which I found ironic, and the Mets trudging in, Castillo, head down, leaving the field in despair. I had to set that scene. You have to not only finish the call; you have to embellish it with descriptions.

Radio is where my idol and mentor Marv Albert shines. In my opinion, he wrote the book for basketball on radio. What I love about Marv's work on radio is his passion. People say Marv is great because he's objective, but that didn't matter that much to me when I was a kid listening to him. What mattered to me was that listening to Marv doing a Knicks game on radio I knew that he was vested in the Knicks, having been a Knicks ball boy, growing up a Knicks fan, being a New Yorker through and through. In fact, he even wrote a book titled *Krazy About the Knicks* (turns out he gave me yet another inspiration). He had true unbridled passion for the Knicks and that appealed to me as a listener. I accepted on faith that he was telling me the truth, but what really appealed to me was his passion.

I remember as a kid listening to a Knicks game during their first championship season. They won a game on a basket at the buzzer by Willis Reed and Marv went berserk. I loved that, because hearing Marv going berserk made me go berserk along with him. That's Marv's passion, and radio brings that passion out.

Quite clearly, Marv Albert is a favorite and a hero of mine, but he's not alone. There are others. I marvel at Bob Costas when he's doing an interview. I know that my mind is not quite as sharp as it was 10–12 years ago, because whose is? I know that some days I have to strive a little harder to find the perfect word. It's just a function of getting older. Costas is a couple of years older than me and he never struggles to find the perfect word. Not only does he always find the words without hesitation, if you listen to him doing an interview there's never any stammering, never any hesitation as he gropes for the right word. That's brilliant in itself, but to find the right word, and most of the time it's the perfect word, is a gift. I just think he's utterly brilliant.

Mel Allen was one of my very early influences, just because I loved the sound of his voice and his passion; it all seems to come back to that for me. Marty Glickman doing football on radio was as good as it got. Marty was a wonderful man, a football and track star at Syracuse who was a teammate of the great Jesse Owens on the United States team in the 1936 Berlin Olympics.

Glickman later became a legend in New York sports broadcasting, the radio voice of the New York Knicks, the New York Football Giants, and later the New York Jets. He had that staccato style that influenced so many who came after him. At the height of his career he was always gracious and supportive of aspiring sports announcers, including this one, and extremely generous with his time and his advice. He became a TV "coach" and worked with me when I started at SportsChannel in 1995.

When I started doing television I wasn't certain where to stand in relation to my broadcast partner. I'd have to make a point and my partner would have to respond to it and I wasn't sure where I should be looking. At the camera? At my partner? Should I look mostly at the camera and steal a glance at my partner? It was a dilemma, and I wasn't comfortable with what I was supposed to do, but Glickman solved my dilemma with just one suggestion. "Think of the camera as a third person in a three-way conversation," he said. He didn't have to say another word. From that moment on, it just clicked with me.

Just about everyone of a certain age who is from New York and who went into sports broadcasting was influenced by, and is a descendant of,

Marty Glickman. Marv Albert was a direct descendant of Glickman, the primary disciple of Marty, and accordingly just about anybody in my general age range who works in New York or grew up here was influenced by Marv.

Among those who worked out of New York, Harry Kalas was great, and of course had those magnificent pipes. He was a great conversationalist and he was beloved in Philadelphia. The great Ernie Harwell in Detroit was simply lyrical and he had some shtick that was cute—"There's a foul ball off to the right of home plate, picked up by a fan from Dearborn"— that's great; I love that sort of stuff. It connected Ernie in a personal way to his hometown listening audience.

As far as I'm concerned, you can't do it any better than Vin Scully. You talk about the penchant for always finding the perfect word, it's a gift, and Scully has it.

Chapter 12
MY ISLANDER PARADISE

In 1995, I came to a crossroads in my life and my career. I was still at WFAN, where I hosted a talk show as well as Mets pregame and postgame shows. I wasn't doing much Mets play-by-play (except for an occasional fill-in shot when one of the regular announcers needed a day off), which still was my ultimate goal, and I was bored. I felt like I was on a treadmill. I'd had enough of talk shows: the same callers, the same questions, the same routine year after tedious year.

Play-by-play always was my first priority. I made a commitment to myself that I would accept the first play-by-play opportunity that came up. I would have been content to spend the rest of my career doing play-by-play either for a team in the NHL or MLB. Either one would be the fulfillment of a dream. My passion was equal for both sports, and it still is.

I will admit to this: starting out I worked much harder at honing my skills in hockey than in baseball, based at least partly on my belief that it's easier from a mechanical standpoint to master the nuts and bolts in hockey than it is in baseball. Hockey is more of a reaction sport. So much of doing play-by-play in baseball is dependent on the background information, which in my early days I didn't have access to. It's easy to say, "There's a ground ball to shortstop," or "there's a foul ball back and the count is 0 and 1," but then what do you say? You need information, you need a background, you need stories, and you have to know people, all things that could only be acquired by being there and doing that, and I didn't have any of that yet.

I therefore set baseball play-by-play on a shelf and came to the conclusion that my only chance to do baseball play-by-play was to develop enough recognition within my own market so that a team would be willing to take a chance, even on a part-time basis, or a once-in-a-blue moon basis to give me a crack. As it turned out later, my connection with WHN and WFAN was the break I needed in order to move into baseball play-by-play. I needed to build off that template as a "talk show guy" with enough of a following so that a team would think, "People know him. He's okay. Let's give him a shot." I'd never have had that opportunity if I was just reading scores.

For now, though, in '95, I was still looking for a full-time play-by-play job, any job, in baseball or hockey. Coincidentally, at the time there was a potential upheaval in the NHL based on rumors that there was a chance the New Jersey Devils were going to move to Nashville. Had that happened, SportsChannel, which owned the television rights to both teams, would have had one team and two announcers: Mike "Doc" Emrick, the Devils' announcer, and Jiggs McDonald, the Islanders guy.

Emrick was still under contract to be the voice of the Devils, but McDonald's contract had lapsed, so SportsChannel made it known that if the Devils moved to Nashville Emrick would switch from the Devils to the Islanders and McDonald would be out of a job. That didn't sit very well with Jiggs, who made some comments that weren't appreciated by the people at SportsChannel. When the Devils' move to Nashville fell through, Emrick stayed with New Jersey, but McDonald was let go. I had been following the situation closely and once I knew all the pieces were in place (Emrick remaining the voice of the Devils and McDonald out as voice of the Islanders), I called my agent and told him to get right on

Here I am with R.A. Dickey as we prepared to leave for a hockey-themed trip to Toronto for an interleague series. R.A., who is from Nashville, is wearing a Predators jersey. (Photo: Shannon Forde, New York Mets)

it. I saw it as my chance to get a play-by-play gig and at the same time simplify my life.

People wonder how I, a lifelong Rangers fan, could work for the Islanders. The fact is I had a history with the Islanders, and despite my love for the Rangers I have always had a soft spot in my heart for the Islanders, as well.

In my freshman year at Queens College, which coincidentally happened to be the first year of the Islanders' existence, I was working for the college radio station and the college newspaper. The Islanders, being the new team to the area, were smart enough to reach out as far as they could to attract attention. They allowed selected local collegiate media to cover their games. That was my opening. The Islanders provided me with a credential giving me admittance to some of their home games with full access to the dressing rooms and everything else that was accorded to the professional working press.

I would bring my tape recorder to the games and go through the motions of doing play-by-play with my partner, Steve Taub, a writer for the campus newspaper, as well as a former player for the Queens College hockey team, just as if we were on live radio. Steve and I dressed the part, looked the part, and respected the club's rules regarding what was and was not off-limits to the press.

After the games, I would join the professional media in the locker room and go through the motions of interviewing the coach and the players, which enabled me to accomplish two things at a very young age (I was only 19 when I started doing this): I became familiar with the inner workings of covering a sporting event, and I formed relationships with many of the people around the Islanders so that as the team evolved and I continued to cover their games I felt very comfortable and welcomed there. I got to know the players so that when I got the job in '95, even though my reputation had been, and still is, as a Rangers broadcaster, I was accepted by such Islanders heroes as Denis

Potvin, Clark Gillies, Bob Nystrom, and Ed Westfall, my first broadcast partner on Islanders games. Their endorsement early on helped my credibility with Islanders fans. Of course there were, and still are to this day almost 20 years later, some Islanders fans that will not fully accept me. And that's great because it speaks to their passion. I understand it and I get a kick out of it because I know that over the years the majority of the fans have been very supportive.

My first few years with the Islanders were difficult. The team was terrible, the fans had no patience with a bad team, and then there was me, coming in from the "enemy." I felt I was navigating a minefield. What saved me was the Islanders front office staff, the alumni, and the people I worked with.

I have had some great relationships with Islanders players and coaches, like Mike Milbury, who was brought in to coach the team the year I was hired to broadcast the games. You might say we were rookies together. Milbury, who was kind of a hockey version of Bobby Valentine, both of them volatile and impulsive and exceedingly bright, has been very supportive of me over the years, for which I am grateful.

My first year with the Islanders was a real culture shock. I had just come from calling the games of a Rangers team that was one year removed from winning the Stanley Cup and now I was with a team that once had produced one of the great dynasties in NHL history with four consecutive Stanley Cup championships in the 1980s, but now had hit the skids and was among the NHL's bottom-feeders.

To emphasize the point, one of my first trips with the Islanders was to Washington, and the bus driver there, a guy named Joe, was a bit of a character: outgoing, brash, and opinionated. He had been driving the visiting teams forever, and everyone knew and liked him. We flew to the nation's capital and the bus met us at the airport and took us to our hotel. Traveling with the Rangers in those days there was always an entourage waiting at our hotel in every NHL city, crowds of people waiting for autographs from stars such as Mark Messier, Brian Leetch, Mike Richter, and Adam Graves. The Islanders had no such stars, so when the bus pulled up to the hotel entrance and the players walked through the lobby there was nobody waiting for them. It was as if the area had been evacuated.

Joe the bus driver, who also was the bus driver for the Rangers and every other NHL team when they played in D.C., saw this reception for the Islanders—or lack thereof—and blurted in a loud voice, "Wow, you guys must really suck!"

I figured Milbury would explode when he heard that. I thought he might haul off and slug Joe the bus driver, or at least give him a piece of his mind. I was wrong. Mike laughed harder than anybody.

Reflecting on those seven years when I was doing the Rangers, it wasn't "my" job, it was Marv Albert's job and I was his backup. That was fine as long as I was doing other things, but it was part of a schedule that was becoming untenable. I never had any time off. I couldn't breathe. My two daughters were very young and I felt I needed to simplify things. Then the opportunity to do the Islanders came up and I not only simplified my life, I finally had a full-time play-by-play job of my own.

When I made the move to the Islanders, I gave up the Mets' pre- and postgame shows, so for a few months during the winter of '95–96 I had no affiliation with the Mets and no involvement with baseball. My deal with SportsChannel was to do the Islanders and a few other things like shows and events. I figured (hoped) they'd also use me to work 20 to 30 Mets games a season, but that's not how things worked out. During the summer of '95, while the Islanders deal was still in the works, I was asked to fill in on a Mets game because two of their announcers, Ralph Kiner and Rusty Staub, were attending the Hall of Fame ceremonies in Cooperstown.

I did the game and I got positive feedback for my work. In fact, a few days later, the executive producer at SportsChannel asked me, "What do you like broadcasting better, baseball or hockey?"

Ralph Kiner has always been one of my favorites, so it was a real honor to be able to host Ralph Kiner Night at Shea in 2007. (Photo: Marc S. Levine, New York Mets)

I knew where he was going. SportsChannel was contracted to do 75 Mets games a season and there had been rumblings that there were going to be changes on the Mets' broadcast team. I figured if I answered hockey I could do a full hockey schedule and also a partial baseball schedule. But if I said I'd rather do baseball, then I would be shutting myself out of all the hockey work and I'd be doing just 75 baseball games. So I took a gamble and said hockey, and sure enough, I not only was the television voice of the Islanders, I also joined Ralph Kiner, Fran Healy, and Matt Loughlin on SportsChannel's Mets TV coverage.

Once more, I was committed to a heavy schedule—but I was young, and I thought to myself, "Here we go again!"

Chapter 13
MANAGERS I HAVE KNOWN

Back when I was hosting the pregame *Mets Extra* show, a regular feature was the manager's segment, which I enjoyed because of the ancillary benefits. It enabled me to form a stronger personal relationship with these men and, at the same time, for me it was a primer on baseball. By dealing with these managers, I not only improved my knowledge of the game, I gained an insight into their thinking and their reasons for making certain strategic moves.

The curriculum was Baseball 101; the managers were the professors and I was the student. I found myself looking forward to those daily sessions, but that wasn't always the case for them. I often found these managers when we first got together to be suspicious, defensive, protective, and defiant. After a time, when I had earned their trust and confidence, these sessions with the manager became a joy as well as a mother lode of baseball knowledge.

My first "professor" was Davey Johnson, who was the Mets manager when I began as host of *Mets Extra* in 1987. He had a profound influence on me in a lot of ways and I had an opportunity to acknowledge that publicly a few years ago. The Mets inducted Davey, Frank Cashen,

Dwight Gooden, and Darryl Strawberry into their Hall of Fame and they held a panel discussion with the four inductees for season ticket holders. I emceed the discussion and in introducing Davey, I said, "I'm not sure I would be broadcasting in the major leagues if it weren't for Davey Johnson and the amount of baseball I learned talking to him every day for the three or four years that we worked together."

My words took Johnson by surprise. He seemed shocked because he never heard me say anything like that and he kind of gave me a look as if he couldn't understand why I said what I did. The fact is, he'll never know how much he taught me, not only about the Xs and Os, but about the inner workings of an organization, the mindset of a manager, how a lineup works, and how a bullpen works, from the conversations we had on and off the air.

At first, I didn't think our relationship was going to work out because Davey wasn't comfortable answering the pointed questions I would ask him. Like most managers, indeed most people, Davey didn't react well to criticism. The prevailing theme of shows like these is that they are generally house organs and it was all going to be happy talk, but my mind-set was that if I was going to be doing this every day, I couldn't shortchange our listeners into thinking that I was any less qualified than any of the beat reporters to talk to the manager. My mandate was to ask the same questions of him that he was going to hear from the writers.

We had one situation after a loss in which a couple of his decisions didn't work out and I asked him about them on the show the next day. He answered my questions but I could tell he was a little uncomfortable. When I turned the tape recorder off, he was hot and got in my face about it. He said, "I'm not going to get into defending my moves after every game."

I was getting a little intimidated because I had never had a situation like that with a manager before. This was different because there was a lot at stake; there was money coming in for sponsorship of the show, so this had to work. I said to him, "You have to hear where I'm coming from. There are fans that are going to be tuned into this show every day and if I'm soft-soaping them and giving them, 'Oh, Davey, this is great, that's great,' after a bad game then there's no credibility and before you know it people are going to stop listening. Nobody's going to take me seriously, and they're going to think even less of you."

Despite my protestations, Davey was adamant about his position and I left there thinking I had failed to get him to see my point of view. But the next day, it was like a switch went off in his head. He was a different person. He started to understand where I was coming from.

The biggest change in our relationship came in July, after WHN morphed into WFAN. Now there was a 24-hour sports call-in cycle on a station that was the flagship of the Mets' radio network, and Davey would drive home and listen to the station after a game and there would be callers saying, "How could Davey do this? How could he do that? How could he bring this guy in?"

He never said so, but I believe that caused the change in Davey. He didn't want to have to defend his decisions the next day, but to his credit the light bulb went off. My guess is that he told himself, "I can deal with listening to this criticism for an hour a night, but if it's going to be 24 hours a day, I'm going to use this show to say exactly why I made the moves I made."

It was obvious that from that point he embraced what I was trying to do. At the same time, I believe he understood me better, he felt more comfortable with me and we were off and running. One day at Shea Stadium, unsolicited by me, Bob Costas came up to me and said, "I have to tell you this is the best pregame show I've heard because you ask the right questions and he answers them. It's not prosecutorial."

High praise from one of my industry's biggest names, and I was most appreciative.

From that point, Davey and I developed a really good relationship. It was mostly Johnson's doing, but I'll take credit for one thing: I learned early on that if I am going to ask a manager to explain some of his decisions, I can't do it in an accusatory tone. I trained myself to present the question thusly: "Seventh inning, you had a left-handed batter coming up, you could have brought in Pitcher A or Pitcher B. Tell me why you chose A over B."

Davey had just won the World Series a few months earlier. He was sitting on top of the world, and he didn't need to be prosecuted for pinch-hitting for someone or for bringing in a pitcher that didn't get the job done. I wanted to make him know that I understood he had options, I just wanted him to tell me why he chose the option he did. And he was okay with that.

Davey's a very bright guy. He's a graduate of Trinity University with a bachelor's degree in mathematics, who was ahead of his time among managers because he used a computer in his preparation and evaluation of players long before it became the fashion. As a player with the Baltimore Orioles, he would hand Orioles manager Earl Weaver eight different batting orders and say, "Earl, any one of these is a winner." His eight batting orders would all consist of the same players but with various permutations and organization of the order in which they were to bat, except for one thing. All eight batting orders had Davey batting fourth. Remember, these were the Orioles of Frank Robinson and Boog Powell—legitimate cleanup hitters.

Because he's so clever, he realized that talking with me on the manager's segment of *Mets Extra* and answering my pointed questions could actually serve a valuable purpose. He could mitigate some of the inevitable second guessing from fans by letting them in on his strategic philosophy. Eventually, our mutual comfort level grew to where I felt confident asking him just about anything, knowing that I would get a candid answer in return.

Before long, Davey Johnson emerged as a valuable resource, enabling me to enhance my understanding of the inner workings of the game.

The best conversations we had were when the tape recorder was turned off. I would ask him questions, many of them no doubt naïve and dumb, but he showed great patience with me. He never seemed to mind explaining how things worked, and believe me, Davy does not suffer fools. He has little to no patience for the uninformed or uneducated.

The most constructive thing I took from him was when he told me, "When you go on the air after a game and you wonder why I didn't use so-and-so, what you don't know is that so-and-so might have had a fight with his wife, or he might have had a little tenderness that we're not going to say publicly. You always have to understand that the manager should get the benefit of the doubt, until you learn otherwise."

I tried always to impart that to the listeners. I always try to include that caveat by saying, "This move doesn't make sense but there may be something we don't know about, but I'll find out when I talk to the manager tomorrow." To his credit, Davey always answered the question. After that he never became defensive when I asked him to explain a move he made, because he knew that I understood what he told me and I always threw that out there as a preemptive strike at callers who might question one of Davey's moves. Davey appreciated that.

I will never forget how much Johnson taught me about baseball. He was the first college professor in my freshman year and he made an indelible impression. I'll always appreciate that. Even now, some 20 years later, he is my professor emeritus, and I'm still learning from him.

He took over the Washington Nationals in 2011 and came in to Citi Field with the Nats for a series with the Mets. For most games, the Nationals played Jayson Werth in right field and Rick Ankiel in center, but this particular night, Davey had Ankiel in right and Werth in center. So I asked him about the flip-flop and in typical fashion, he rolled his eyes and threw his arms into the air and said, "Let me ask you something. What am I going to do when—"

I stopped him right there and said, "Don't ask me. I don't know your team. That's why I'm asking you."

When he finally settled down, he explained that at the time he was thinking ahead because the Nationals weren't sure if their phenom

Bryce Harper was going to make the team, but if he did he was going to have to play a corner outfield position because he's not a center fielder, at least not yet, so Davey wanted to see if Werth could play center field. It all made sense, but how was I supposed to know that, and that's exactly what I told him. But that's Davey. He likes to say, "How can you not know what I'm thinking?"

I did learn one thing that night. All those years later, Davey Johnson hadn't changed a bit. And by the way, in 2012 his Nats won the NL East and Harper played plenty of center field.

Winning 108 games and the World Series in '86 and winning 100 games and finishing first in the National League East two years later made Davey Johnson bulletproof. But when the Mets got off to a slow start in '90, there were rumors that Johnson had lost control of the team and his job was in jeopardy.

Davey Johnson is a rebel, and he was saying things on the show that irked general manager Frank Cashen to no end. On May 27, the Mets lost to the San Diego Padres 8–4, their third loss in their last four games, dropping their record to 20–22. Two days later in Cincinnati, Johnson was fired and replaced by his third-base coach, Bud Harrelson. It was yet another example of how the front office was beginning to dismantle what made the '86 Mets what they were. Cashen wanted a sycophant and Davey could never be thought of as anything close to that. On the other hand, Harrelson, a company man forever, was just what Cashen was looking for.

It was clear to everyone around the team that Cashen, tired of Davey's public comments questioning his manner of running the team, had been looking for a reason to get rid of Johnson and the slow start gave it to him. In Harrelson, Cashen had someone he believed he could control, someone who was a hero of the Mets miracle run in 1969 and someone who was a favorite among fans and the media. Nobody doesn't like Derrel McKinley Harrelson. He is everybody's beloved Buddy, the revered shortstop of a championship team.

Buddy was clearly hired to be the anti–Davey Johnson. Cashen had enough of Johnson's independence, his brashness, and he wanted a company guy. And Buddy was unabashedly a company guy.

My relationship with Harrelson, which was always a good one and still is to this day—I consider him a friend—changed when he replaced Johnson as manager and on the manager's segment of *Mets Extra*. At first we had a lot of fun with the show because Buddy was more comfortable around a microphone than Davey was. Buddy was a different kind of communicator than Davey was. Davey was understated and Buddy was garrulous, effusive, fun-loving, and upbeat.

After a while though, Buddy started growing uncomfortable with some of the lines of questioning on the manager's show. He wanted to control the editorial part of the show. His orders were pretty much don't rock the boat. When the Mets moved Bob Ojeda to the bullpen in '90 it was a big deal. The fans had a lot of questions, but when it came time to do the manager's show, Harrelson said, "I don't want to talk about Ojeda."

I protested. I said, "We've got to. It's the back page in every newspaper in the city tomorrow and it's all the callers are going to want to talk about. It's a big story around the team."

But Harrelson refused to talk about it. I said, "I don't care how you answer it, but I have to ask it. I at least have to bring it up."

He said, "I don't want to discuss it."

I said, "Here's what I have to do. When I open the show, I'm going to say, 'We acknowledge the big story today that Bob Ojeda has been sent to the bullpen, but Bud Harrelson does not wish to discuss it, so here now is the manager's report."

Bud was fine with that, but it put him in a bad light. He finally got to the point where he quit doing the show because he didn't like the fact that I was asking him pretty much the same questions everybody else was asking him after games. He thought the show should be a cheerleading session. I was friendly enough with him then that I sat with him and tried to tell him what the perception would be if he ducked the issues. I said, "I understand you're not doing this as a personal thing against me, but people are not going to understand that. They're going to look at this and say you're scared, you're weak."

Contrast Harrelson's approach to the manager's show with that of Davey Johnson, who couldn't care less what the front office wanted and thrived on the controversy.

A perfect case in point is that in the first month of the 1987 season the Mets activated Roger McDowell, who had started the season on the disabled list because of a hernia. That night I opened the manager's segment with something like this:

"Davey, you got Roger McDowell back tonight. How does that affect the rest of the bullpen?"

"Howie, Frank Cashen made a dumb move today."

We were doing the show on tape and when I heard that my thought was, "This is great, just go," but when we had finished the show I thought this might not sit well with Cashen, so let me give Davey the chance to reconsider what he said. I turned the tape recorder off and said, "If you're not comfortable with that and you want to do it again, I'm fine with it. I have the time to do it over."

Davey blew his top.

"Why would I want to do it again?" he practically screamed at me. "I said it because I wanted to say it. I wanted him to hear that."

Harrelson would never say something like that—not in a million years—and that's what Cashen wanted and why he brought in Buddy to replace Davey.

After he replaced Johnson, Harrelson revived the Mets and had them in contention until the final week of the season, but the next year the team collapsed, won only 77 games, finished fifth, and Harrelson was fired.

I don't think Harrelson ever aspired to be the manager of the Mets. He took the job because he was such a company man and the company came to him in its hour of need. I feel sure Buddy would have been content to continue as third-base coach. Had he done so, he could have become the Mets' equivalent of Frank Crosetti, who spent 37 years in uniform with the Yankees as a player and coach. Harrelson was and is a tremendous teacher and a fabulous coach.

But then getting fired by the Mets may have been a blessing in disguise for Harrelson. It led to him getting involved in the ownership of a very successful independent team, the Long Island Ducks, and today, I'm pleased to say, Bud is a happy man. His Ducks won the 2012 Atlantic League championship.

To replace Harrelson the Mets chose Jeff Torborg, a nice man, a New Jersey native, and a Rutgers alumnus with no previous connection to the Mets. But he had attracted a great deal of attention by taking a bad White Sox team and finishing second in the American League West in '90 and '91.

I never worked with Torborg on the air because while he was the manager I was in my two-year exile from *Mets Extra*. New general manager Al Harazin didn't want me involved in a manager's show after what happened with Harrelson, but the situation was temporary, as was Harazin's tenure as GM. Sadly, so too was Torborg's term as Mets manager. In '92 the Mets finished 72–90, 24 games out of first, and then Jeff was fired 38 games into the '93 season, after the Mets compiled a 13–25 record. Within a few weeks, Harazin was out, too. I knew Torborg because even though I wasn't hosting *Mets Extra*, I was still doing my talk show on WFAN and that took me out to the ballpark often. I will always remember him for delivering one of the great lines in Mets history.

After he was fired by the Mets, Jeff went into broadcasting, first with CBS radio and then with Fox television. In those days, inductees in the Mets Hall of Fame were depicted with busts displayed outside the Diamond Club on the fourth floor in Shea Stadium. To get to the press box, one would have to walk past the Diamond Club, and the first time Torborg did so after he was fired, he noticed the Hall of Fame display and commented, "I should be in there."

He paused, waiting for someone to ask the inevitable, "Why?"

"Because I'm the biggest bust they ever had."

To replace Torborg the Mets selected Dallas Green, who had pitched ever so briefly for the Mets (four games in '66 with no record), but who had managed the Phillies to a World Series title and later served as general manager of the Cubs, for whom he acquired Hall of Fame second baseman Ryne Sandberg. Green came with a reputation for being tough and rigid, baseball's John Wayne. He built that persona and thrived on that reputation. He seemed to rule by intimidation. By 1994, I was back in the good graces of the Mets, and was not only doing Mets Extra but was also frequently filling in for Bob Murphy doing radio play-by-play. In 1996, I began doing Mets play-by-play on TV for SportsChannel.

For some reason, Green was convinced that I was out to get him. Eventually, during his tenure, I was doing Mets games on cable television and Gary Thorne was doing the games on regular TV. I think what happened is that Gary, who is a little more caustic in his comments than I am, made some remarks that were critical of Green and more than likely when it got back to Dallas, whoever told him about those remarks attributed them to me instead of Thorne. Or Dallas just assumed it was me.

One night in 1996, after a long excruciating game between the Mets and Cardinals in St. Louis that the Mets won in extra innings—the kind of game that could drive a manager nuts—I was in Mike Shannon's restaurant with some of the broadcasters. At some point I left my seat to go to the men's room and to do so I had to pass the bar where Dallas was sitting with umpire Joe West. In passing Green I said, "Sometimes I think they can't pay managers enough."

Dallas did a double take and with a snarl said, "Well that's surprising to hear considering you've been trying to get me fired all year."

His comment came out of the blue and shocked me. "What?" I said.

"Ah, don't worry about it," Dallas said, and I continued to the men's room.

My thought at the time was that either Dallas was attributing remarks made by somebody else to me or he had had a few drinks and it was the alcohol speaking. My mistake was failing to nip the thing in the bud. I take all the blame for not trying to repair that unpleasantness in the immediate aftermath. I should have gone to him the next day and attempted to clear the air. By not doing so I was going against a vow I made to myself early on that if I criticized a player and wasn't sure if that player was teed off at me, I would make certain to show up in the clubhouse the next day and stand well within view of that player so that if he had a problem, he could come to me and confront me about it.

This proactive strategy has met with mixed results. In 1990, the Mets experimented with Keith Miller, an infielder by trade, playing center field. This did not go well. Miller had trouble adjusting to a position at which he had no experience, and the fans were not patient at all. Every misplay was magnified, particularly on my postgame show, where callers were free to vent; and vent they did.

Invariably, I would try to defend Keith by pointing out that it was only April, and even though the early returns were not promising, he deserved at least a bit of a grace period while he tried to learn a difficult position at the Major League level.

One night during that early stage of the season, Miller was actually the Mets' star of the game, and agreed to join me for the usual postgame clubhouse report. I was in the booth and he was in the clubhouse on a headset, so I couldn't see his expression, but his tone of voice gave away the fact that he was angry about something. I asked the questions and he gave the answers, but this usually pleasant, talkative fellow was uncharacteristically curt and brief with his responses. At the end of the interview, after I said thanks, he mumbled "Yeah," and that was the end of it. No "You're welcome," or "My pleasure," just a sour-sounding "Yeah."

Obviously, something was wrong. After the show, I went downstairs to the clubhouse, but Keith had already left. I found Jay Horwitz, the Mets' public relations director, who told me that Miller was mad at me because he heard that I had been critical of his defensive work on the air. I just laughed, and told Jay that I had actually defended him, and Miller's messenger had gotten it wrong.

I explained this to Keith the next day, and in fact I gave him a copy of the on-air exchange in question so he could hear for himself. He could not have been nicer or more apologetic in person, which didn't surprise me. He was always a classy guy, and remains so today in his role as a player agent. I still bump into him once or twice a year.

Incidentally, the center-field experiment did not last long. By the end of April 1990, the Mets picked up Daryl Boston from the Chicago White Sox and Miller's days as a center fielder were over.

You may have noticed a common thread between the Dallas Green story from St. Louis and the Keith Miller episode: players, managers, and coaches rarely hear what we say about them in real time. Generally they hear about it from a friend or a family member. Often the message is badly distorted by the time the player gets it, although one of my more puzzling confrontations was with a player who not only heard the message right, he actually said the same thing I did—and still, he got mad at me.

Brett Butler was a solid Major League outfielder who spent most of the 1995 season with the Mets. One Saturday afternoon he had an awful game, misplaying a couple of balls in the outfield and struggling at the plate, leaving several runners on base. On my postgame show I said that Brett Butler had just played the worst game I had ever seen him play. It was not an exaggeration, and in the next morning's *New York Times*, Butler was quoted having said the same thing about himself. Believe me, you didn't have to be Branch Rickey to come to that conclusion. Nonetheless, when I arrived in the clubhouse at Shea Stadium that day, Butler was looking for me.

He said his wife had heard what I said about his performance on the air, and that she was at once furious and embarrassed. When I reminded Butler that he had described his play the day before exactly as

I had, he was not the least bit mollified. He said that as one of his team's announcers I had an obligation to look for the positives and gloss over the negatives, and although I explained that we generally do look for something positive to say, never mind that we have an obligation to tell the truth to a sophisticated audience, the fact that he had said almost exactly the same thing about himself as I had really made his reaction kind of silly. He didn't see it that way, thinking I must have said more than I was admitting to.

I offered to give him the tape so that he could hear for himself, and he actually said, "I'll take the tape, but it's not going to change my opinion." Why I even bothered getting him the tape I'll never know, other than to further clear my conscience, but my strategy at that point was to wait for him to apologize. He never did. Later that season, he was traded to the Dodgers. I ran into him once or twice along the way in the ensuing years, and although we were cordial, we never had much of a conversation. He might not even have remembered the incident. However, I did. It simply reinforced my thinking that some people are just not cut out to play in New York.

Anyway, back to Dallas Green.

A month after he made those comments in St. Louis, Green was fired and I never had a chance to talk to him about it. But I'm pleased to say that I run into Dallas frequently when the Mets play in Philadelphia and he's been great. We have pleasant conversations. There has been no carryover to that one unpleasant incident.

In his two full seasons and two parts, Green failed to improve the Mets. They won 229 games and lost 283 under Green, who was fired near the end of the '96 season, and along came a baseball tornado otherwise known as Bobby V.

Chapter 14

BOBBY V.
(AS IN VOLATILE,
VOCIFEROUS, VINDICTIVE,
VICTORIOUS, ETC....)

Let's establish something right up front: I am a Bobby Valentine fan. On August 26, 1996, Bobby Valentine succeeded Dallas Green to become the 16th manager of the New York Mets and the 10th since I began broadcasting their games. He took over a team that was in the throes of its sixth straight losing season. Over the next six years he would win 536 games. In 2000, he guided the Mets to their first World Series in 14 years. His managerial tenure with the Mets covered 2,228 days; not one of them boring.

Bobby V. was flamboyant, imperious, perceptive, tyrannical, sagacious, egomaniacal, perspicacious, irascible, inventive, exacting, fearless, demanding, charming, and arrogant. He managed with a twinkle in his eye and a chip on his shoulder. He was daring, combative, and argumentative. But he was never dull.

Looking back years later at Valentine's regime, I realize I underutilized Bobby as a resource. In the middle of the tumult of a baseball season you can understand how, especially considering the grind that he was in, some of his Napoleonic condescension would come out. But there also were the times when you were able to get him away from that and he was just unbelievable.

For all his braggadocio about his knowledge of the game, he's not wrong about that and he proves it every day. I learned a lot of baseball from Valentine and I could have learned a lot more had I been a little less worried about how he'd respond to my questions and just take at face value that here was a potential wealth of information. I didn't tap into it as much as I could have and should have.

Here's an example of why it was hard for me to approach Bobby more casually in an attempt to pick his brain. In September '98, the Mets were in contention for the wild-card when they played a four-game series in Houston. It was an unbelievable series. Three of the four games went into extra innings, and the Mets won the series, three games to one.

In the final game, the Astros were leading 2–0 in the ninth inning and were one out away from nailing down the win when Mike Piazza hit a three-run home run off Billy Wagner to give the Mets a 3–2 lead. However, Brad Ausmus' home run in the bottom of the ninth tied it. They went into extra innings and the Mets won on Todd Hundley's two-out home run in the top of the 11th.

After the game we flew home by charter. As I boarded the plane, on my way to my seat, I had to pass Valentine sitting in his customary location in the front of the plane. As I walked past him, I stopped, looked at him, and said, "How great is this?"

Valentine looked up at me, arched his eyebrows, and straightened up in his seat in surprise. For a moment he was speechless, and then he said the strangest thing.

"Thank you for enjoying it."

If I could have predicted 1,000 responses to "How great is this?" no way would "Thank you for enjoying it" even had been on the list.

The next day I said to him, "You sounded surprised that I would have enjoyed yesterday's game; that I would get a kick out of how great these games have been."

And his response to that was also strange.

"Nobody ever comes over to me after a game and says, 'Nice game, Skip!'"

I thought, "That's not really what I was saying. It wasn't about 'Nice game, Bobby.'" I wasn't complimenting him for his strategy, I was just expressing my appreciation for the game and because what I had witnessed was great theater. This is not a criticism of Valentine, it's on me that I found it hard to feel I could go up to him and spontaneously start kicking around ideas about strategy. I didn't feel confident enough that it would be a normal conversation rather than a "Why would you ask me that?"

The thing about Valentine is that he has a tendency that if you say "A" he's going to explore every aspect of "B" because that's what Bobby is: a contrarian. I have discovered over the years that there are a lot of inordinately bright people who are contrarians by nature and, in my experience, Valentine is at the top of the list. That's just their DNA. Part of their makeup is they want to prove themselves right and you wrong no matter how sound your premise or your thinking might be. That's my arms-length view of Bobby Valentine. I think it's just a manifestation of innate competitiveness.

One time, soon after he took over as manager of the Mets, I think it was '97, Bobby made a couple of changes in a game on a getaway day in Cincinnati that looked like he had wasted a player. Gary Cohen was doing the games on radio and I was doing television. Later, Gary and I were sitting next to each other on the charter flight back to New York and, as we often did, we were rehashing the game. I asked him if he thought Valentine had wasted a player and Gary, who doesn't miss anything, agreed. He told me he even mentioned it on the air, which I also did and apparently so did longtime Reds' broadcaster Marty Brennaman. After a while, Valentine, who sees, hears, and knows everything, approached Gary and me.

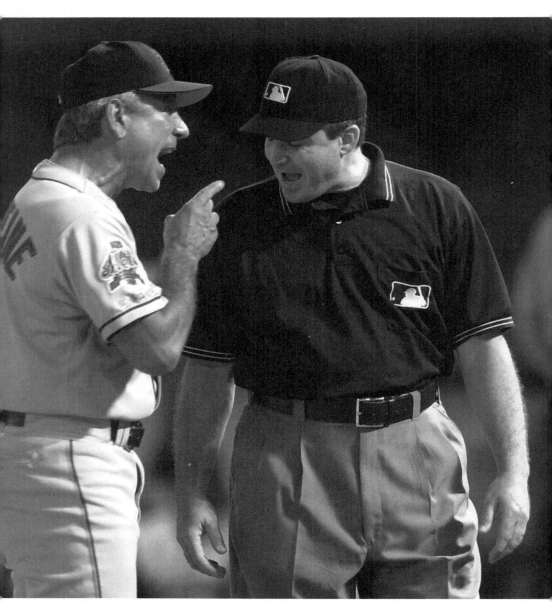

Bobby V. in his environment, arguing with Ed Rapuano after being thrown out of a 2002 game. (AP Images)

"All right, what did you guys think of that move?"

I couldn't run from it because I said it on the air and I figured Bobby had to have heard that I did, so I said, "I thought you wasted a player."

Then he turned to Gary.

"What about you?"

"Same thing."

"All right, let me explain," Valentine said smugly.

He then went on to give us this lengthy convoluted explanation that I didn't understand or agree with then, and I still don't. Satisfied that he had made his point he returned to his seat. Moments later John Franco, who had been observing this scene, came to us and said, "What did Bobby tell you?"

We tried our best to explain Valentine's circuitous route to the logic of his move. Franco just looked at us, smiled, and said knowingly, "He screwed up!"

With Valentine you never knew what you were going to get from one day to the next. He could be effusive one day and taciturn the next, forthcoming one day and contentious the next. As a case in point, I offer the evening of June 9, 1999, the Mets in an interleague game at Shea Stadium against the Toronto Blue Jays. With the score tied 3–3 in the top of the 12th, one out and a runner on first, Mets catcher Mike Piazza was called for interference and the Jays batter, Craig Grebeck, was awarded first base. Bobby V. blew his top and argued so vociferously, umpire Randy Marsh had no choice but to run the Mets' manager out of the game.

Understand that when a manager is ejected, he'll find some way to continue in control of his team. He might repair to his office, watch the game on television and communicate with his coaches by telephone. Or he might hide in the runway between the dugout and clubhouse, out of view of the umpires, fans, and television cameras, and issue his orders from that vantage point.

On this day, Valentine tried a different approach. Moments after being ejected, he could be seen lurking in the corner of the dugout wearing sunglasses and a Groucho Marx mustache, which were hardly sufficient disguises to conceal his identity and were easily picked up by the TV cameras and later distributed and transmitted nationally.

The National League office took a dim view of Valentine's actions, fining him $5,000 and suspending him for two games. Some thought he was guilty of showing up the umpires and making a mockery of the game and that what he did was an embarrassment to the game and to the franchise. Still others saw the stunt as an indication Bobby was taking leave of his senses, having some sort of breakdown. I strongly disagree. I know I'm in the minority here, but I absolutely loved what he did and I said as much on the air, which got me criticized in some corners for not recognizing the seriousness of the situation.

I thought I knew where Bobby was going with that stunt. The week before, the Mets had been bogged down in an eight-game losing streak. They were playing poorly. The payroll was high, the expectations were high, and when you have a high payroll and high expectations in New York, you don't have the luxury of playing poorly for any length of time without all kinds of attention and pressure being foisted upon you. When I saw Bobby in his sunglasses and mustache, I remember thinking, "This is great. This is super. What he's doing is designed to deflect the fact that the team is in a bad streak, to take the heat off the players and loosen everybody up." That's how I interpreted it and I was pleased to hear after the fact that Bobby said that was exactly his intent.

When I talked with players about the incident, they were just as split as everybody else. Some saw it as I did: a means of lightening the mood. Others thought it was Bobby being Bobby, putting the focus on himself, fostering the notion that everything always came back to him. He loves the stage, and he knows exactly what he's doing at all times. I believe there's not one move that man makes that's not calculated.

Someone once said that whenever Bobby wins a game he looks like he wants to go out to the pitcher's mound and take a bow in front of everyone in the ballpark. Bobby also has a tendency to fall on the sword, though, which he did at the end of the '98 season when the Mets had the wild-card in their pocket and collapsed in the last week. As the wild-card was getting away from them, Bobby said something to the effect of, "They should fire me if we don't make it."

Some players saw that as another example of a manager taking the heat off his players. Others were critical of his choice of words and his timing. "What's he have to say that for?" they asked. "It's not about him, it's about us."

There seemed often to be a disconnect between Bobby V. and his players. Some swore he had a sincere affection for them. Others believed his motives were less than pure. There never is a middle ground with Valentine. Some like him, some dislike him, but nobody's indifferent.

I came to truly appreciate Valentine's brilliance as a manager when I witnessed it up close and personal in the National League Championship Series of '99 and '00.

Bobby made a move in Game 5 of the '99 NLCS against the Braves that convinced me how shrewd a manager he is. Seventh inning, score tied 2–2, the Mets down three games to one and facing elimination. On the mound for the Mets was right-hander Turk Wendell, with Dennis Cook, a left-hander, and Pat Mahomes, a right-hander, warming up in the bullpen.

With one out, Bret Boone was hit by a pitch and was replaced by Otis Nixon, a pinch-runner. After Chipper Jones struck out, Brian Jordan, a right-handed hitter, was at bat, and Ryan Klesko, a big left-handed hitter who always seemed to get big hits against the Mets, was on deck. On the second pitch to Jordan, Nixon stole second, leaving first base open and a count of 2–0 on the batter. With that, Valentine brought in Cook, the left-hander, with instructions to throw two more intentional balls to

Jordan and walk him to put runners on first and second. That brought Klesko up to bat. Now Valentine had the upper hand. Cook had pitched to the mandatory one batter (Jordan), so he could be removed from the game, which was exactly what Bobby V. had planned (Bobby wanted Klesko out of that game). When Brian Hunter, a right-handed hitter, was announced as a pinch-hitter for Klesko, meaning Braves manager Bobby Cox took the bait, Valentine went to the mound again and removed Cook, the left-hander, in favor of Mahomes, the right-hander.

Cook was livid. He left the mound fuming, TV cameras following him and lip readers catching him spewing a barrage of expletives. He could not understand why you would bring him in to intentionally walk a hitter and then lose him for the rest of the game.

As it turned out, Mahomes walked Hunter, but got out of the inning by inducing Andruw Jones to hit a fly ball to left field. Valentine had maneuvered to get his desired matchup. He got Klesko out of the game and the Mets won in the bottom of the 15th when Robin Ventura hit one over the fence with the bases loaded but was officially given a "grand slam single" because he was mobbed by his teammates and wrestled to the ground before ever reaching second base.

The Mets lost Game 6 and were eliminated, but Valentine clearly outmaneuvered Cox in the series. The next year, in the NLCS, he totally outfoxed Tony La Russa when the Mets advanced to the World Series. Two years in a row, Valentine undressed Bobby Cox and Tony La Russa, two certain Hall of Fame managers who, between them, won 5,232 major league games.

In both series, Valentine got just about every matchup he wanted, and that's what managers will tell you: half of managing, if not more, is getting your matchups. He's the best bench manager I've ever seen. If I were in charge of a team and had to win one game there's no manager I've seen that I would entrust with handling the game strategically over Bobby Valentine. He's just brilliant. But he also likes to let you know it.

I suppose it sounds like I was initially intimidated by Bobby Valentine, and maybe I was, but there is no "maybe" about the fact that I was in awe of his knowledge of the game. I was in awe of his ability to see everything and anything happening on the field and be prepared with a counter for any situation that arose. It was clear he thoroughly enjoyed the competition and mind games with opposing managers, and he taught me an enormous amount of baseball, whether he realized it or not.

Bobby Valentine was a spectacular and much-ballyhooed three-sport star in baseball, football, and track at Rippowam High School in Stamford, Connecticut. He must have been a tough kid to like when he was young. A great-looking guy, great athlete, champion ballroom dancer, there seemingly was nothing he set out to do that he couldn't accomplish. As insufferable as people perceive him now, imagine what he must have been like as a 17-year-old.

He was recruited by the University of Southern California, who planned to groom him as the replacement for O.J. Simpson. Instead, Valentine chose baseball and signed with the Los Angeles Dodgers, who made him their top pick in the June 1968 amateur draft.

A brilliant baseball career was cut short when Valentine suffered a broken leg in 1973. He bounced around to the Angels and Padres before being traded to the Mets in a deal for Dave Kingman as part of the so-called "Midnight Massacre," the night in '77 when the Mets traded Tom Seaver.

Valentine joined the Mets coaching staff under manager George Bamberger in 1983 and two years later was hired as manager of the Texas Rangers, where he stayed for eight seasons. He managed the Chiba Lotte Marines in the Pacific Division of the Japanese Baseball League before returning to the Mets as manager of the Norfolk Tides, their affiliate in the AAA International League. He succeeded Dallas Green as manager of the Mets for the final 31 games of the '96 season.

Over the next couple of years it became quite evident that Bobby Valentine was a remarkable judge of talent. He instinctively, after a sufficient sample, could identify those players who fit and those who did not fit his vision of his team, and the ones who didn't were not long for the Mets.

In 1996, three Mets players enjoyed career years: Lance Johnson, Todd Hundley, and Bernard Gilkey. Johnson set the franchise record for most hits in a season, Hundley for most home runs in a season, and Gilkey had one of the best all-around seasons of any Mets player in history. Still, for a variety of reasons, Valentine determined that none of those players fit into his long-term plans, and before too long, they all became ex-Mets. The kicker to the story is that none of the three ever approached their 1996 success with their subsequent teams. Valentine had been right about all three of them.

In 2000, Valentine's Mets won the National League pennant with an outfield of Benny Agbayani in left field, Jay Payton in center field, and Timo Perez in right field. These were all legitimate Major League players, but I don't think they necessarily fulfilled anyone's vision of a championship-caliber outfield. Bobby Valentine felt otherwise, and his confidence became his vindication.

The Mets finished the '96 season in fourth place with a record of 71–91. The next year, Valentine guided them to 88 wins and third place in the National League East, and by '99 they were a serious contender, winning 97 games. In '00, they won 94 games and made it to the World Series against their crosstown rivals, the Yankees.

The Yankees had struggled to the finish line and barely edged the Red Sox for the division title, and then struggled to beat Oakland and Seattle in the playoffs.

In the World Series the Yankees got a jump on the Mets by winning Game 1, a 12-inning spine-tingler in Yankee Stadium that would set the tone for the entire Series, by a score of 4–3. The game was scoreless in the sixth when Mets leadoff man Timo Perez was thrown out at the plate attempting to score on a double by Todd Zeile. While Perez has been roundly criticized for the gaffe, some have blamed Zeile, who hit the ball off the top of the left-field fence and thought it was out so he went into his home run trot. Instead of following the flight of the ball as he should have, Perez was watching Zeile. When he saw Zeile go into his home run trot Perez also thought the ball was out and he didn't bust it home until it was too late. The Yankees would go on to take a 2–0 lead in the bottom of the inning.

What I could never excuse was that here was this guy, Perez, who was playing in Japan when the Mets found him and who was in the minor leagues until the Mets brought him up in late August that year and this kid, who had been in the major leagues only a few weeks, was taking something for granted in the World Series in Yankee Stadium.

The Mets took a 3–2 lead with three runs in the seventh and missed an opportunity to add an insurance run in the ninth when Perez batted with one out and a runner on third. I was talking with Valentine the day after the World Series, and he confided that if Perez had gotten ahead in the count in that at-bat, Bobby was going to put on the squeeze play.

If there is one criticism I have of Bobby's managing it's that he fell in love with the squeeze play and used it so much that he became predictable with it. You could usually tell when it was coming. Perez fell behind in the count and Bobby must have anticipated his predictability. With a count of 0–1, a pitchout is a strong possibility, so Valentine took the squeeze sign off. Perez wound up grounding out, the Mets failed to score and the Yankees tied it in the bottom of the ninth and won it in the 12th.

There's no telling how things might have changed if Timo Perez had scored that run on Todd Zeile's double or if the Mets had been able to squeeze home that insurance run. Valentine insists that the outcome of the World Series would have been different if the Mets had won Game 1, and I have no reason to doubt him.

So instead of the Series being tied, the Yankees went up two games to none with a 6–5 victory in Game 2, the game in which Mike Piazza broke his bat, with the barrel eventually ricocheting off of pitcher Roger Clemens, who fired it like a spear in Piazza's direction. Both benches emptied but order was restored before there was mayhem. Some said

Piazza and Clemens have words after Clemens threw Piazza's broken bat head in his direction during the 2000 World Series. Said Clemens, "I thought it was the ball." Right. (AP Images)

the Mets should have used the incident as a rallying point and fought the Yankees. I disagree. Suppose Piazza attacked Clemens and both of them were thrown out of the game, maybe even suspended for the Series? That's not a fair trade. The Mets would lose their offensive leader, a .324 hitter with 38 home runs and 113 RBI, and the Yankees would lose a pitcher that might get into only one more game.

The Mets won Game 3, but lost Game 4 by one run and lost Game 5 by two runs when the Yankees scored two in the top of the ninth, and the World Series was over.

In just four years, Valentine took a team that had won 71 games and helped restore Mets pride by winning 367 games, bringing them back into contention and reaching the World Series. And yet in his six-plus seasons as manager of the Mets, Bobby V.'s finest hour came not from something he did on the field but something he did off the field.

It came in autumn '01, after the collapse of the two World Trade Center towers on 9/11. A city was dropped to its knees and was in desperate need of a pick-me-up, and Valentine rolled up his sleeves and went to work to help provide it.

As a sidebar, I was the emcee of the Mets' annual Welcome Home Dinner that spring and I was seated next to Bobby. Mayor Rudy Giuliani, who has this reputation of being a huge Yankees fan, which he has never denied, was to be the featured speaker and when Giuliani got up to the podium, Valentine whispered to me, "They should boo him!" And then a few months later, Valentine and Giuliani were joined at the hip in the recovery after 9/11 and Bobby's opinion of Giuliani changed. He no longer viewed him as the enemy.

In this time of devastation and of need, Bobby stood tall and came through like a champion. He worked tirelessly at Shea Stadium, which was being used as an emergency staging area for rescue workers, and he befriended children who lost parents during the attacks and invited those children to join him as his guest at the World Series and other celebrity-studded baseball events.

At first, it was tough dealing with Valentine on a daily basis because he'd be on his guard. He didn't like to be criticized and he'd challenge you if he thought you were second-guessing him. But we eventually found a common ground and a meeting of the minds and I came to love working with him. Now when I see him I make it a point to pick his brain. And he's always receptive, accommodating, and agreeable, which makes me regret all the more that I didn't take full advantage of that opportunity earlier.

His failed 2012 season as manager of the Boston Red Sox notwithstanding, I firmly believe that Bobby Valentine still has plenty to offer Major League Baseball. If a daring owner is willing to give Bobby full reign of his team's baseball operations, perhaps as a general manager/field manager, allowing him (paraphrasing Bill Parcells) to shop for the groceries and cook the meals, that team could go for quite a ride.

One thing is for certain…it wouldn't be dull.

Chapter 15
MORE MANAGERS

Probably the worst thing that happened to Art Howe was that the Mets made him their manager *after* Bobby Valentine.

Art Howe wasn't Bobby Valentine, couldn't be Bobby Valentine, didn't want to be Bobby Valentine, and he didn't try to be Bobby Valentine.

If Bud Harrelson was the anti–Davey Johnson, Art Howe was the anti–Bobby Valentine. It should have been a clue to Mets management that if Harrelson failed as Johnson's successor, Howe had no chance to succeed only 13 years later as Valentine's successor.

To replace Valentine, the Mets' first choice was Lou Piniella, who would have been a more suitable replacement for Bobby V. Piniella had many of the same fiery, swashbuckling qualities as Valentine. In addition, he had a New York pedigree from his years as a player and manager with the Yankees, and he was a popular figure among fans and the media.

Unfortunately for the Mets, Piniella was under contract as manager of the Seattle Mariners, who were reluctant to let him go. However, they would consider letting Lou out of his contract if the Mets paid them compensation. Someone, the Mariners said, like this young shortstop who had played the previous year in Port St. Lucie and Binghamton in the Mets' farm system, a kid named...um...er...Reyes, first name Jose. Yes, he would do just fine.

Nothing doing, said the Mets, who then turned their attention to other options, among them Art Howe, whose only connection to the Mets was a little-known bit of trivia. He was the last batter Tom Seaver faced before being traded by the Mets to the Reds. (Playing for the Houston Astros, Howe flew out to deep left field, Seaver had his final win in his first go-round with the Mets, and a few days later Tom was on his way to Cincinnati.) But Howe had done a wonderful job managing the *Moneyball* Oakland Athletics. In four years, from 1999 to 2002, he had guided the Athletics to 383 wins, two first-place and two second-place finishes, and three postseason appearances.

Nevertheless, in retrospect, Howe was simply the wrong guy with the wrong team in the wrong town at the wrong time.

Because he was not good copy (following Bobby Valentine didn't help) and he didn't win, Art Howe has been given a bad rap by Mets fans and the media. I get angry at the way he's portrayed by some who make him out to be a bad guy, which is the furthest thing from the truth. Because he didn't win, does that make him a bad guy? He takes an unfair beating in New York. It was a bad couple of years for the Mets and Howe might not have been the right guy for the job. Let it go with that.

Forget about Art Howe as manager. He is one of the finest people I've ever met in my years in baseball. I first realized that Art was a regular guy and someone I would enjoy talking to and being around early in his tenure. On Mets charter airplanes, Art would walk through the plane and sit down with guys—not only players but broadcasters, trainers, media, anybody in the team's traveling party—and begin a conversation. He would say, "Hey, how ya doin'? How's your life going? What's new with you?"

It wasn't just baseball, it was life in general. He made you feel like you were important to him and he cared about you. That's what I like about him. He's just a nice, easygoing, and wonderful guy. One time we were on the road and things were crumbling, the team was falling apart, the Mets were in an austerity period and Art wasn't getting the help in terms of player procurement that he hoped for. I was walking past the manager's office and Howe called me in and looked at me with sad eyes and threw up his arms and said, "Howie, what am I supposed to do?"

I had never experienced a relationship with a manager where he would do something like that, kind of cry on my shoulder, and I felt so bad for him because he deserved better. Whenever I interviewed him, Art was always cooperative and never sensitive to the second-guess, just the easiest guy in the world to talk to.

There was never anything pretentious about Howe. His idea of a night out was to take his wife to a little neighborhood Italian restaurant called Aunt Bella's in Douglaston, Queens, a place my friends and I loved and frequented for years. When he told me that, it made me think, "This is my kind of guy. Nice and normal." And that's exactly how he played out in the two years he was managing the Mets.

Unfortunately, as Leo Durocher once famously said, nice guys do finish last—or last and next to last in this case. Saddled with a team comprised of past-their-prime stars like 30-somethings Roberto Alomar, Mo Vaughn, Mike Piazza, Tom Glavine, and Al Leiter, 40-something Johnny Franco, and still-not-ready-for-prime-time youngsters David Wright and Jose Reyes, Howe won only 137 games and lost 186 and was fired after two years.

Having missed out on Piniella when Howe was hired, the Mets made certain to replace Howe with someone that did have a New York history and had been a local hero. Willie Randolph had spent 24 seasons with the Yankees, 13 as an All-Star second baseman, a key component to three pennant winners and two World Series championships, and another 11 years as a coach. My relationship with him dated back to when he was a player and I was a kid working first for SportsPhone and later as a reporter for WCBS radio. After 15 or 20 minutes of chasing Reggie Jackson, Graig Nettles, Lou Piniella, and others around the Yankees clubhouse with my tape recorder, I often would take refuge at Willie's locker to get a nice, calm, rational answer to my questions. It was like his locker was "base."

(If you remember the old street game Ringolevio, that's what I called Willie—"Base.")

I consider Randolph a friend and here's all you need to know about him to gain some insight into his character and how I feel about him. After three successful seasons as manager of the Mets in which he had a winning record each year and won one division title, on June 17, 2008, his fourth year on the job, with the team under .500 at 34–35, Willie was fired. Randolph was hurt by the firing, as any manager would be. Nevertheless, on the morning of the last day of the season, with the Mets still clinging to a chance for a playoff spot, I got a call from Willie. The Mets were no longer his team, he was gone, but he called to wish me luck and to wish the Mets luck.

"I know it means a lot to you and everybody else over there," he said. "Good luck and I hope you guys win today."

That showed a lot of class coming from someone who obviously was still hurting from being fired only a few months before. He could have been bitter. But he took the time before the last game to send along his good wishes. I thought that was great of him.

Like most managers, Randolph experienced some highs and lows in his three-plus years as manager of the Mets. He had never managed before, still, in his first year he took over a 71–91 team and improved it by 12 games, finishing tied for third place, seven games out of first.

In '06, Randolph's second season, the Mets won 97 games, won the National League East by 12 games, swept the Los Angeles Dodgers in three games in the division playoffs, and faced the St. Louis Cardinals for the National League pennant.

With the series tied three games each, it all came down to Game 7 in Shea Stadium on Thursday, October 19, 2006, and with the score tied 1–1, it came down further to the ninth inning. In the top of the ninth, Yadier Molina belted a two-run home run off Aaron Heilman, and the Mets came up to bat in the bottom of the ninth three outs away from elimination.

Jose Valentin and Endy Chavez hit back-to-back singles to start the inning and the Mets had the tying runs on base with Cliff Floyd coming to bat. A lot of people thought Randolph should either have had Floyd bunt or pinch hit someone who was a better bunter than Cliff to move the runners over. Instead, Willie was unwilling to give up an out. What he wanted was for Floyd, who had hit 34 home runs the previous season, to turn a fastball around and with one swing win the pennant with a three-run homer.

The Cardinals' pitcher, Adam Wainwright, was just 25 years old, and I could imagine Randolph's thought process being something like this: "I'm looking at a young pitcher who's in trouble. Maybe he's a little tight and he'll try to throw a fastball over the plate on the first pitch to get ahead in the count, and Cliff, a good fastball hitter, might sit on it, crank it, and let's celebrate."

But Cliff struck out and Jose Reyes lined out to center field. Paul LoDuca drew a walk to load the bases for Carlos Beltran, the Mets' best hitter, who had blasted 41 homers and driven in 116 runs that season. And Beltran looked at a third strike. The Mets' season ended with Beltran's bat on his shoulder.

Naturally, after the game and for weeks after the season, there was much second-guessing of Randolph for not bunting with Floyd and criticism for what some observers saw as confusion and a lack of communication in the dugout for what Floyd was ordered to do.

I really wish the Mets would have won for Randolph, but they didn't. It was an unpleasant off-season for Willie, and it only got worse the next year when, after leading the National League East by seven games on September 12, the Mets, in one of the worst collapses in baseball history, which Willie presided over, lost 12 of their final 17 games and finished a game behind the Phillies and out of the playoffs.

Many people believe that when a manager suffers such a monumental collapse, you can't bring him back the following year. I didn't see it that way at the time, but it became clear by the middle of June that Randolph had lost his team, and he was fired.

Enter Jerry Manuel, who had been Randolph's third-base coach.

Manuel had the gift of gab. By contrast to Randolph, Jerry's pregame sessions were a breath of fresh air. Willie was very guarded and defensive and Manuel seized the opportunity to use the pregame press conference as a stand-up act. After about a week of his pregame press conferences, those of us around the team on a daily basis talked about how entertaining he was. At one point I told him in private, "I really appreciate your candor in these press conferences."

And Jerry looked at me and started laughing in that guffaw of his— he had a great laugh—and he said, "Well don't believe everything you hear."

"I didn't say I believed it," I replied. "I just said I appreciated it."

As a strategist, I thought Manuel was mediocre at best. I rate him as a run-of-the-mill manager, undistinguishable from the masses of managers in any way, which is evident by his record, losing records in his two full seasons, '09 and '10, fourth-place finishes both years, 23 and 18 games out of first place, respectively.

When it came time to choose a successor to Jerry Manuel, the people's choice was Wally Backman, who had managed successfully in the minor leagues and impressed a lot of baseball people with his knowledge, his strategy, and his leadership. But the Mets took the conservative route and selected Terry Collins, a baseball lifer who managed 11 years in the minor leagues and six years with the Houston Astros and Anaheim Angels with moderate success, who was known for his attention to detail and his organizational skills.

It appeared Collins was hired to keep the seat warm for Backman, honing his managerial skills in the Mets farm system. The choice of Collins did not dazzle anybody, me included. I was wrong.

As a strategist, most managers are alike, and Terry is no different than most. He's neither going to embarrass himself or distinguish himself with some revolutionary form of strategy. After all, how many Bobby Valentines, Billy Martins, Tony La Russas, and Gene Mauchs are there who are innovative and a cut above the rest strategically? The "rest" are still pretty big so it's not an insult to be in that group; a lot in that group have won World Series.

Most managers know when to bunt and when to hit-and-run. The most important thing for a manager is how he deals with his players. Is he a leader of men, can he get the most out of his players, can he get his players to buy in, to play for him?

When it comes to those things, I have come to the point where I now give Terry Collins high marks. I also put him in a class with Art Howe as a person of character, compassion, and sensitivity. And I put him on

Here I am with Mets manager Terry Collins. (Photo: Marc S. Levine, New York Mets)

the top of the list among managers I have known in organization and attention to detail.

Collins is a no-nonsense guy. Ask him a question and you get a direct answer. He has no agenda. He does not play games or mislead people. And you can talk baseball with him all day. It wasn't long after he arrived in 2011 that I anointed Terry as among my favorites of the 14 Mets managers I have covered since 1976. I hope he has a long run.

Chapter 16
A DAY IN THE LIFE

I am a notorious, devout, and inveterate creature of habit; always have been, always will be. As a result of this addiction, on game days I like to have a routine to take me up to the first pitch or the drop of the puck. It's an obsession (maybe even a fear) I have about being properly prepared so there are no surprises when it's time to go on the air.

Over the years I've modified my typical hockey day-of-the-game routine considerably. Most games start at either 7:00 or 7:30 PM and teams generally hold a "skate" or light practice the morning of a game. The players wake up, go to the rink, work out, go back home (or to the hotel if they're on the road), take a nap, get up, go back to the rink, and play the game. To me, this is lunacy. I have often wondered, for example, why professional boxers will train in the morning or the afternoon for championship fights that usually start at 10:00 or 11:00 at night. Doesn't that upset their body chemistry?

For many years I dutifully attended these hockey day-of-the-game skates, thinking there would be some value in witnessing them or fearing I would miss something important if I failed to attend. Gradually, I came to realize that anything I would get, or miss, at these 10:30 AM sessions I could easily obtain at 5:00 PM that night. For me, attending a morning skate became nothing more than false hustle.

Legend has it that the morning skate was the brainchild of a coach who wanted to make certain his players were forced to wake up early enough in the morning to dissuade them from staying up too late the night before. I'm not sure how effective this coaching ploy has been, but I'll be willing to bet that somewhere along the way a player actually has gone straight to the morning skate from his previous night's activities. The late Pat Burns, who coached the New Jersey Devils to a Stanley Cup championship, was no fan of the morning skate and made many of them optional, when he bothered to hold them at all.

Burns once said, "If the Rolling Stones have a concert at 7:30 at night do you think they go to the arena at 10:30 in the morning, sing a few songs, go back to the hotel to take a nap, and then go back to the arena for the concert?"

This goofiness is not limited to hockey. For years NBA teams have had a game-day routine that includes a "shootaround," which isn't endorsed by many players. One notable unwilling participant of the game-day shootaround was Wilt Chamberlain. When Bill Sharman coached the Los Angeles Lakers he installed the practice of a morning shootaround on game days, presumably for the purpose of getting the players limbered up, but more likely for the same reason as the hockey skate. Wilt wanted no part of it. "Coach," he told Sharman, "you've got me once a day. Do you want me in the morning or at night?"

Needless to say, Chamberlain didn't make too many morning shootarounds, or how would he have been able to find time to entertain (by his estimate) more than 20,000 ladies?

Instead of wasting my time at a morning skate, I spend the day of a hockey game reading the out-of-town newspapers, getting the game notes and other tidbits off the Internet, making notes, memorizing numbers, and then heading to the arena, generally between three and four hours before the opening faceoff. Once there, I talk with whomever I need to in order to wrap up my preparation, and once that's done, it's showtime. About an hour before game time I will voice a "tease," a

12-second introduction to the game that will air before we go on camera. Once the tease is recorded it's time for a quick bite, and then the fun starts when they drop the puck.

Baseball requires a completely different form of preparation from hockey. While in hockey we're seeing a different opponent for every game and rarely are games played on consecutive days, a baseball schedule is played in multi-game series. Consequently, most of the preparation is done before the series opener and the next few days are much easier.

As a result, the day of the first game of a series in baseball is a whirlwind. If the team is at home, I will rise early, have breakfast, get in a one-hour workout, shower, and then repair to the office in my home to read everything I can about that night's opponent. Looking through out-of-town newspapers on the Internet is a must in order to keep up with teams from around the majors. It can be very time consuming, but my goal is to have it all done in time for lunch, and then it's off to the ballpark.

Obviously, most baseball games these days are played at night. On the rare occasions when there is a day game, the preparation is accelerated. I might miss my daily workout and do most of my research at the ballpark and not at home.

It's on days like these that I find myself appreciating what the pioneers of baseball broadcasting, such as Mel Allen, Red Barber, Harry Caray, Jack Buck, Bob Prince, Ernie Harwell, Curt Gowdy, Vin Scully, Harry Kalas, and the Mets' own Lindsey Nelson, Bob Murphy, and Ralph Kiner had to endure. None of them had the advantage of information from the Internet or the avalanche of statistical matter provided by the Elias Bureau when they began broadcasting, and most of them never even had notes or batting averages prepared by the teams, at least not in their early days.

When the Mets are at home, I get to Citi Field at about 3:30 in the afternoon for a 7:00 PM game. Hopefully, the starting lineups are available at that time so I can get a head start on filling out my scorebook. Manager Terry Collins is as punctual as any skipper I've been around. He knows how to make the most of his time. When he says he will hold his pregame media briefing at 4:00, he's not kidding. He's in the interview room at 4:00 on the dot and his sessions are informative and productive.

Once Terry is finished with his briefing, I try to spend time talking to a few players, the opposing manager, or some of the broadcasters

In the broadcast booth with New York mayor Michael Bloomberg and my partner at the time, Tom McCarthy. (Photo: Marc S. Levine, New York Mets)

and writers from the opposing team, in an effort to get background information on who has been playing and pitching well in recent days, or any tidbit that might fit into the broadcast.

From 5:00 to 6:00 PM I can be found in the radio booth feverishly working on the primary tool of my trade, my scorebook. I prefer having everything in front of me as opposed to shuffling through papers to find something I need, so I make copious notes in my book. That gives me easy access to the information I'm seeking. Early in my career, I would fumble through media notes and other random pieces of paper to find a particular stat or bit of information, but that didn't work well for me. By the time I found what I was looking for I was as disheveled in my head as the papers were on my desk. I knew I had to get my act together and establish a system that worked best for me and that's what I did.

After I have my scorebook filled out, the last hour, between 6:00 and 7:00 PM, belongs to me. I'll have dinner and relax so that my mind is clear when we go on the air at 7:00. That hour between 6:00 and 7:00 is one of my favorite times of the day. There's always someone interesting to spend time with in the media room: a former player, a scout, a veteran broadcaster, or newspaperman. The baseball stories are often enthralling, a veritable history of baseball, and if the fruit salad is cold and the weather is warm I'm in a good frame of mind to start a broadcast. Warm fruit salad and cold weather? That's another story!

My routine for games on the road is very similar to home games. There's nothing more depressing to me than being cooped up in a hotel room during the hockey season when the weather is so cold it precludes outdoor exploration. Baseball season usually means the weather is good. I love to walk round the various cities where the Mets play. Lunch and a casual stroll is always a highlight of my day on the road. San Francisco with its hilly streets and beautiful scenery and Chicago with its hustle and bustle are as good as it gets, and to me the best walking cities in the National League.

Weather has a lot to do with dictating my moods. I love summer and abhor winter, so when the sun is shining, the weather is warm, and I'm at the ballpark, even after all these years, I still feel like that little kid in the general admission seats at Shea Stadium anxiously awaiting the game's first pitch. The best part is that now I get to call that pitch on the air. I guess that's what people mean when they say I'm "living the dream."

Chapter 17
TAKE ME OUT TO THE...

To those of us fortunate enough to make our living as sportscasters, there's a popular saying: "We do the games free; we get paid to travel."

I'm a strong advocate of this philosophy.

To be sure, if one is in his twenties, the travel is not only broadening, it's as much fun as you can imagine. So, too, is the lifestyle. But once you settle down to raise a family, the time away from home can often be painful.

My two daughters, now adult young women, grew up knowing their dad would come and go for days, even weeks, at a time. That was the normal order of things for them. But that didn't make it easier for any of us to take when birthdays or other special occasions rolled around and I wasn't there to celebrate those events with them. We all learned to simply deal with the absences and have come through those difficult early years mostly because Barbara, my wife, did an amazing job being both mother and father at times. But trust me when I say life on the road is not all fun and games.

For me, the best part of traveling always has been the opportunity to enjoy the various and sundry ballparks and arenas, particularly the older ones that I grew up seeing on television. Unfortunately—or in some cases

The greatest team a man could ever be a part of: (left to right) my daughter Alyssa, me, my wife, Barbara, and my daughter Chelsea.

happily—most of those relics are gone, but I thought I'd discuss some of my favorites.

Because I am an unabashed sentimentalist and very much a baseball traditionalist, I get a special thrill out of working in Chicago's Wrigley Field, Boston's Fenway Park, and Los Angeles' Dodger Stadium.

Whenever I enter Wrigley Field, my mind immediately goes back to 1969, the Bleacher Bums, and Ron Santo clicking his heels before the Mets broke his heart and the hearts of his teammates and Cubs fans.

Dodger Stadium serves as a shrine to Vin Scully and Sandy Koufax and provides a glimpse into my youth every time I walk across the field on the way to the team bus after a game. Oddly, especially after a day game, I find myself angling toward first base and imagining how Joe Pepitone must have felt when he lost Clete Boyer's throw from third base in the background of white shirts in the pivotal play of Game 4 of the '63 World Series.

A rare visit to Fenway Park never fails to jolt my mind back to '67, when I rooted hard for the Red Sox to complete their "Impossible Dream," going from ninth place in the American League the year before to the pennant in one of the greatest races in baseball history. As a 13-year-old, I had bonded with Red Sox fans while dreaming of what it would be like for my Mets to experience such a turnaround. Two years later, I had the answer.

The old places are special for the history and memories they evoke, but that hardly makes them ideal for doing one's job. We broadcasters are quite particular about what makes for the best working conditions (they vary from broadcaster to broadcaster). As you might imagine, we're all pretty fussy. My personal pet peeve is an aversion to cold weather. I hate being cold, so the first thing I look for in a booth is heat. Obviously if the booth is heated, that's a good thing, but it doesn't mean my search has ended.

Almost as important to me as heat is a window that can open and close easily. Such a device and engineering marvel allows me to feel as if I am in total control of the heating situation and I'm good to go (wind is a broadcaster's enemy as well). Citi Field, the Mets' new ballpark and my home away from home for some 80 days in the six months from April to September, passes the test in both vital (for me) respects.

The ideal situation is for the booth to be installed with two windows that open in both an upward and a downward fashion, one on each side of the booth for each announcer to control as he wishes, rather than one long window that slides from side to side. Like normal people, sportscasters are creatures of comfort, and in addition to keeping out the cold, those windows come in handy on days when the wind is blowing in and all of your paperwork—statistics, notes, promos and commercials to be read, etc.—is about to go airborne and wind up in Connecticut. It goes without saying that once summer arrives, air conditioning in the booth is a must, even for one who has an aversion to being cold. There's just no need to overdo it.

In inspecting a radio booth, size matters. The wider the better! Not that I don't like my broadcast partners, but I like having as much elbow room as possible in order to organize my reference books, scorebook, papers, beverage, snack, and any other toys I might want to play with during a rain delay or a game pitched by Steve Trachsel, Hideo Nomo, or Miguel Batista, three of the tortuously slowest pitchers whose games I have ever broadcast.

Also important in a broadcast booth is proximity to the field. In that category the parks in Washington and Pittsburgh, in my opinion, finish in a dead heat for last place. Those new ballparks make life difficult for broadcasters by placing the booth so high it becomes a challenge to differentiate one pitch from another. Those vantage points replicate the view from Shea Stadium's upper deck. Great for a fan, not so much for a broadcaster. While you can easily discern a slow curveball from a Stephen Strasburg fastball at that height, most pitches look the same from such a high perch and the broadcaster has to work a good deal harder to identify them accurately. (True confession time: even if you put most broadcasters in a lawn chair behind the home plate umpire, there's still a great deal of guesswork involved with calling pitches. While we all strive for perfection, I have often heard a pitcher, catcher, and batter describe the same pitch differently.)

Once when the Mets were scheduled for a rare visit to Detroit for an interleague series, Gary Cohen, my broadcast partner at the time, advised me to bring my baseball glove with me on the trip. I replied that I thought we were a little old for that, but he informed me that broadcasters needed a glove for self-defense because the broadcast booth in Tiger Stadium was so close to the field and hung so far out that foul balls hit straight back turned broadcasters into hockey goalies. I quickly discovered that even a glove was inadequate. I could have used a mask and chest protector.

Now that you have my specifications for the perfect broadcast booth, what else is important? Well, broadcasters are likely to drink a good deal of water during the course of a three-hour baseball game, so use your imagination. A bathroom! Hopefully close to the booth!

Once more, Pittsburgh's PNC Park, an absolutely gorgeous facility, forgot the broadcasters. The closest men's room to the booth in PNC Park is a $10 cab ride away, so an announcer has to make certain his partner is there to cover for him when nature calls or have wheels like Jose Reyes. Oh, yes, it's also desirable that the broadcast booth be close enough to the press room so that a beverage or snack is well within reach.

Needless to say, although they don't yet have the tradition and history of their predecessors, for the best in state-of-the-art facilities, the newer ballparks have it all over the older ones. Wrigley Field, built in 1914, is a classic, but it has no elevator, its broadcast booths are tiny and narrow and have windows that are installed and removed once and only once a season, and is the least comfortable place to work in the major leagues. Forget the Curse of the Billy Goat. Build a new broadcast booth in Wrigley Field, and then maybe, *just maybe,* the Cubs will finally win a pennant. (By the way, what kind of an idiot brings a goat to a baseball game? Based on that alone, the curse is justified!)

Working conditions at Fenway Park, which opened in 1912, are just as bad as Wrigley Field, but Dodger Stadium, which was opened in 1962, is still clean, beautiful, well-cared for, picturesque, and comfortable, after half a century.

Following is one man's opinion for the best broadcast facilities in baseball outside of New York:

1. Minute Maid Park, Houston. I absolutely love that place unconditionally. They did everything right when they built it. On top of that, the staff is helpful and courteous, and there are no rainouts or delays. Too bad the Astros are moving to the American League and taking their ballpark with them.

2. Great American Ballpark, Cincinnati. It feels like I'm working in my living room when I do a ballgame there. The booth is cozy and comfortable, and the ballpark is underrated, too.

3. Miller Park, Milwaukee. Gigantic booths, great bratwurst (though not as good as those at old County Stadium, which mixed in about 50 years worth of grease from the grill in every delicious bite), and a chance to visit with the great Bob Uecker, who will no doubt show you the baseball he hit for his first big-league foul ball.

4. AT&T Park, San Francisco. Okay, so there's no up and down window in the broadcast booth, but I can put up with a lot of inconveniences in one of the greatest American cities. Also just the aroma of those garlic fries makes you feel as though you've eaten some and it doesn't cost you a calorie!

5. Citizen's Bank Park, Philadelphia. The entire press setup is superb, their announcers are great to hang out with (especially my former partner, Tom McCarthy), and if they had heat in the booth they would rate much higher.

Chapter 18
PRATT FALL

In spring 1999, Tom Seaver and I shared the duty as co-emcees of the Mets' "Welcome Home Dinner" at the New York Hilton hotel that annually serves to launch the season. During the speaking portion of the program, Seaver and I alternated introducing the players, all of them seated at a double-tiered dais.

At one point, Seaver introduced Bobby Jones, a right-handed pitcher from Tom's hometown of Fresno, California.

"This next guy, this pitcher, I love him," Seaver began. "He and I have a lot in common. We both went to the same high school. We both grew up in the same hometown. And between the two of us we have three Cy Young awards."

Typical Seaver whimsy; of the three Cy Youngs Tom was talking about, Jones contributed none. It was Seaver's idea of a joke as well as a little harmless needle to a guy he knew well. There was a smattering of nervous laughter in the audience as some caught on to the joke and others were embarrassed for Jones. But that was the theme of the dinner, to have fun with it.

We continued introducing the players and we finished with the regulars and then we came to the bench players. It was my turn and the next player to be introduced was Todd Pratt. I wanted to build these players up, to make it sound like each one of these bench guys had played a vital role in the team's success the previous year (when they won 88 games and just missed winning the wild-card), and was counted on to do the same in the upcoming season. This is how I began my introduction of Pratt:

"One thing about this team is that it has depth. It's been proven time and time again over the years that you can't win without depth. Every great team has depth. Even the Three Stooges had Shemp."

I paused to accept the strived-for laughter and then I presented Todd Pratt, backup catcher, who stood and took a bow. When the introductions were completed and dinner was served, Pratt approached me and in a menacing tone said, "We're done, dude!"

"What?"

"I get it," he said. "You give all those great introductions to the stars we have here but you come to the scrubs and I'm some stooge?"

I said, "You gotta be kidding!"

I thought he *was* kidding. When I realized I was wrong (for one frightening moment I thought he was going to haul off and slug me in front of Mets officials, his teammates, and some 1,000 fans) it took 10 minutes for me to convince him (I think) of the purity of my intentions. He begrudgingly accepted that I was merely joking and the reference to Shemp was not a slur but a compliment.

Apparently his teammates teased him mercilessly, even called him Shemp, but some also pointed out that I was complimenting him and that seemed to change everything. For about a month, whenever I saw Pratt he couldn't have been nicer. He'd give me a big hello when he saw me, even held elevator doors for me. He went far out of his way to be friendly.

At the next Welcome Home Dinner he was still with the team and John Franco came over to me and said, "Hey, you gonna introduce Pratt?" (I did, sans Shemp references.)

With the Mets, Pratt played behind Mike Piazza, which meant that he wasn't going to get to play a great deal, only 276 games and

555 at-bats in five years. But his teammates loved him and he had his moments. One was a walk-off home run off Matt Mantei of the Arizona Diamondbacks in the bottom of the 10th inning of the fourth game of the 1999 National League Division Series that clinched the series for the Mets.

Another came later in the postseason, Game 5 of the National League Championship Series against the Atlanta Braves, with the Mets down three games to one in the series and 3–2 in the game. Pratt drew a bases-loaded walk to tie the game and Robin Ventura followed with a game-winning drive over the wall. So excited was Pratt that instead of circling the bases, he jumped on Ventura's back. The result was that Ventura's home run was negated, but the good news was that the Mets won the game with what would come to be known as a "grand slam single."

Since I began doing play-by-play of Mets games in '96, my rough estimate is that I have interacted in one way or another with some 400 players who wore the team's orange and blue uniforms. That's more than 40 percent of the number of all the players in Mets history.

Some of those 400 Mets, like Todd Pratt, were unforgettable for their great success on the field or for one play or one at-bat. Some were unforgettable for their shocking failure. Some were unforgettable because they were off-beat characters, quick-witted, intelligent, articulate, quotable, and just good guys. Some were unforgettable because they were difficult, surly, uncooperative, mean, nasty, and just a plain old pain in the behind.

And some were just forgettable.

Clearly, I neither have the space here nor the total recall to be able to give you a profile of all 400 Mets, but I have culled and sorted out the ones who are to me especially interesting and I profoundly offer my apologies to any present or former Met that feels slighted. I hereby present, in no particular order, my observations on some particularly memorable Mets.

When I think about Todd Pratt and the incident at the Welcome Home Dinner, I can't help but also think of John Olerud, who was sitting closest to me during the event and got the biggest laugh out of the whole Pratt-Shemp thing. He was hysterical.

What I remember most about Olerud is that he was exactly what you would expect him to be if all your knowledge of him came simply from watching him play. In other words when you watch John Olerud at bat or in the field and you watch his demeanor, you see his professionalism, his approach. There's an intellect to the way he hit. There's a smoothness to the way he defended. There's an almost inconspicuousness about his persona. He never was flamboyant in any way, not demonstrative in any way, and if you added that all together and surmised what that would create in his personality away from the game, it was exactly the same. He's not gregarious, but he is really pleasant. He's smooth, but with that smoothness came an intellect. John is a very bright guy.

The thing everybody remembers about Olerud is that he wore his helmet in the field, which made him the butt of some undeserved ridicule. The fact is, Olerud suffered a brain aneurysm in 1989 and he promised his parents (his father is a doctor) that he would always wear the helmet in the field. The helmet also made Olerud a central figure in a legendary baseball story that was circulated widely but turned out to be more apocryphal than factual.

The story, as perpetuated by one of the Mets clubhouse employees, is that in '00, after Olerud left the Mets, he signed a free agent contract with his hometown team, the Seattle Mariners. That same year, the Mariners also signed Rickey Henderson, who had played with Olerud on the Mets. According to legend, upon hearing that Henderson, who knew nobody's name, would be joining the Mariners, this Mets employee said, "Wouldn't it be funny if when he gets to Seattle and he sees Olerud wearing the helmet, he goes up to him and says, 'Hey, that's funny. I played with a guy in New York that also wore his helmet in the field'?"

It never happened, but somebody overheard the Mets employee telling the story, believed it to be true (it was credible, after all), and passed it along and it wound up appearing as fact in *Sports Illustrated.*

Mike Piazza and his Mets celebrate with John Olerud after Olerud's walk-off single in a May 1999 game. (AP Images)

Olerud played for the Mets for only three seasons, from 1997 to 1999, but he made his mark, on and off the field. In those three years he hit 63 home runs, drove in 291 runs, batted .306, and played an outstanding first base. In '98, Olerud finished second in the National League batting race by nine points behind Colorado's Larry Walker with an average of .354, still the highest single-season batting average in Mets history. Somehow though, I feel that Olerud has become perhaps the most underrated player the Mets ever had.

I found Jeff Kent to be consistent…consistently difficult. What bothered me about Kent was that if I was doing a postgame show and he was one of the stars of the game and I wanted him to be on the show, unfailingly he would come on. He'd be downstairs and he'd put the headset on and say, "JK here, ready to go." He almost never turned me down if he was one of the stars of the game. But he hardly ever acknowledged me other than that.

I think he did the pregame and postgame stuff because he liked getting himself out there. His appearance on the TV show *Survivor* lends credence to the theory. He even had a kids corner that he did on SportsChannel. But I never found him warm. He was strange. Never mind a handshake, to get a hello out of him was an effort and that bothered me. Don't turn it on one day and then treat me like dirt the next.

He came to New York with a built-in predisposition against all things New York. Even though he was born in California, he lives in Texas and he liked to portray himself as this big old cowboy who was never going to get along with New York, no matter how either party might have tried. The problem was, he didn't try.

Eddie Murray, who spent two seasons with the Mets (1992–93) and is in the Hall of Fame, was like that. His teammates loved him wherever he went. And in a couple of postgame shows I did with him, he was great. I found him engaging, thoughtful, and interesting. But the next day I'd see him and he'd treat me like someone he had never seen before. Hey, we spoke only 12 hours ago.

Kent had been drafted by the Toronto Blue Jays, but in his rookie season for Toronto in '92, he was traded to the Mets for David Cone. It turned out to be a terrible trade for the Mets, who seemed not to make up their mind if Kent was a third baseman or a second baseman. They shifted him back and forth between the two positions until they finally gave up on him and traded him to the Cleveland Indians for Carlos Baerga and Alvaro Espinoza, an even worse trade than the one with Toronto.

In parts of five seasons with the Mets, Kent hit 67 home runs and drove in 267 runs. He was young and just coming into his own. Had the Mets kept him, he might have been a perennial All-Star for them. He would wind up playing 17 seasons for six different teams, make the All-Star team five times, be voted National League MVP with the San Francisco Giants in '00, and finish his career with 377 homers, 1,518 RBI, and a career batting average of .290, which look like Hall of Fame numbers to me.

I've thought a lot about Kent's credentials for the Hall of Fame. When I look at the numbers and the position he played and I look at Ryne Sandberg's numbers and Bill Mazeroski's numbers, he fits the bill. And I'm all for defense; it kills me that Keith Hernandez is not in the Hall of Fame. His defense sets him apart even if his offensive numbers (162 homers, 1,071 RBI, .296) don't. With Keith, the voters look at the position and say he should have had better numbers for his position. I don't agree with that.

With Kent, I have to look at who's in and how does he compare with them? Bill Mazeroski is in, albeit via the Veterans Committee. Ryne Sandberg is in. Wonderful player, but Kent's got better numbers. Joe Morgan? He was a base stealer and a better defender than Kent, but Kent has 109 more home runs than Morgan, 385 more runs batted in, and his lifetime batting average is 19 points higher than Morgan's.

Bottom line? I don't have a vote, but if I did, I would begrudgingly vote for him because I don't think in good conscience I could keep him out just because I thought he was a pain in the butt.

Every once in a while you can be wrong about a person, misjudge him or prejudge him unfairly. For me, that was the case with Gary Sheffield, who signed in '09 as a free agent with the Mets, his eighth and last team in an often brilliant, sometimes controversial 22-year career.

I had interviewed Sheffield once on the telephone for my talk show, but I had never met him. From what I'd heard about him and read about him I was predisposed not to like him. I had decided he was like Jeff Kent and Eddie Murray: arrogant, difficult, surly, uncooperative, and disingenuous. I couldn't have been more wrong.

I found Sheffield to be a much nicer guy than I anticipated. He came with a reputation of being selfish, and that did manifest itself once or twice with the Mets, but overall I found him to be great. Great guy. Great teammate. The guys seemed to really like him and that surprised me about him. I thought that in the various stops he made he had alienated a lot of people. I found him to be honest almost to a fault, bluntly so.

The reason I did the telephone interview with him was because there were stories that when he played for the Brewers, he had deliberately thrown some balls away to force a trade. That's a no-no; it may also have been cause for banishment from baseball or, in the least, a suspension, so when I asked him, point-blank, "Did you make errors intentionally to force your way out of Milwaukee?" I was shocked when he said, "Yeah." He didn't hide from it or run from it, and I appreciated his honesty.

When he got to the Mets, I found him to be really pleasant. You could ask him anything. He never ducked any controversy and once he said something that produced a backlash, he wouldn't back down, issue any denials, or claim, as so many do, that he was misquoted or misunderstood. The fact that he didn't hide from things and owned up to them I found very impressive. It made me respect him all the more.

As difficult as Kent and Eddie Murray were, Cliff Floyd, Mike Cameron, Jason Bay, and Tom Glavine are just the opposite. I think of Floyd and Cameron as 1 and 1A because they were teammates with the Mets in '04–05 and became the closest of friends, practically inseparable

on the road. They were also like two peas in a pod as far as demeanor and character, at the top of my list of all-time favorite Mets.

In my preparation for a game, I always like to have a few ideas in mind as I head for the ballpark. Who do I want to talk to before the game? What do I want to make sure to get in during the broadcast? In other words, just try to organize whatever I can about something that is, by its very nature, so extemporaneous.

One day I showed up for a day game after a night game, dog tired from the long night before and the short morning, and completely without an idea to pursue for the upcoming game when I walked in the clubhouse. In situations like that I found that Cliff Floyd was my go-to guy. So this day I went to his locker and said, "Cliff, I have nothing today. Give me something." And Cliff starts telling stories, pertinent stuff, funny stuff.

As a veteran, Floyd was a leader in the clubhouse during his four seasons with the Mets. Lastings Milledge came up from the minor leagues as a young player that the Mets believed had the talent to be a superstar. Unfortunately, he also came up with an attitude and the reputation for being difficult. Soon after he arrived, Floyd took it upon himself to grab Milledge by the arm and march him over to where they had the video in the clubhouse. He sat him down and said, "Here's what you do. You sit down here, here's who's pitching today. You watch this and you study the pitcher's tendencies."

Floyd and Cameron were interchangeable parts, both bright, both introspective, both funny. Just great guys who were great for a clubhouse. Everybody on the team really liked both of them. They could get along with anybody. In a big-league clubhouse made up of diverse personalities from varying cultures from all parts of the world, there aren't many players you can say that about. Too often there are factions, players splintering off into little groups, going their separate ways. But Floyd and Cameron had the ability to break down those factions. I would be hard-pressed to think of anybody who didn't like Cliff Floyd and Mike Cameron.

The ice-breaker in my relationship with both Bay and Glavine was hockey. I could always talk baseball with any Met, but there haven't been many with whom I could engage in talk about hockey. Along with baseball, it really is one of my great passions, and it's a sport that I've been associated with professionally for almost 30 years as a broadcaster.

Jason Bay comes from British Columbia, which means he probably was skating as soon as he could walk, or before. He's a nice guy and very bright and I feel for him because since he joined the Mets he's had such a tough time with injuries and a lack of production. He signed a huge contract and for whatever reason—maybe he was pressing to try to live up to the contract—he has not produced like the Mets thought he would.

This is a guy who once batted .306 for the Pittsburgh Pirates. He drove in more than 100 runs and hit more than 30 homers twice with the Pirates, once with the Boston Red Sox, and again in '08, which he split between the two teams, but hasn't come close to those numbers since he signed a rich, four-year free agent contract with the Mets. It's sad. You can't help but root for him because he's such a nice guy; the most patient guy I've ever seen under the circumstances. Here's a player that has terribly underperformed since he became a Met. He's been on the disabled list a few times, so he's had to answer a lot of questions about how his rehab is going, and you know it's killing him to have to do it.

Sometimes players need to know that we in the media appreciate them, and Bay is one guy I appreciate because he'll stand at his locker as long as you want him to, answering all the questions that he must hate having to deal with, but he's never nasty, never condescending, never anything even resembling rude. He'll acknowledge being sick and tired of answering the same questions over and over, but at the same time he'll tell you that he knows you have a job to do so he's there as long as you need him to be. I really appreciate that about him and so I root for Bay to find what he once was.

I was and still am very fond of Tom Glavine, and not only because of our common love of hockey. I found him to be very bright, very easy to talk to, and very opinionated. He grew up in Billerica, Massachusetts, and was a big hockey star in high school. He wanted in the worst way to go to Harvard to play hockey. There was one spot open on the Harvard hockey team, but they needed a defenseman so they gave it to a guy named Don Sweeney, who became a terrific defenseman for many years with the Boston Bruins.

The irony is that Glavine was a center iceman. If he had been a defenseman, he probably would have been accepted to Harvard, and baseball would have had one fewer 300-game winner. Glavine was so highly regarded as a hockey player that he was drafted by the Los Angeles Kings out of high school, ahead of future NHL stars Brett Hull and Luc Robitaille. He signed with the Atlanta Braves instead and embarked on a Hall of Fame career.

One of my biggest thrills since I have been with the Mets was to broadcast Glavine's 300th win on August 5, 2007, against the Cubs in Wrigley Field.

Glavine played 22 seasons in the major leagues, pitched in 682 games, won 305 games, started eight World Series games, won two Cy Young awards, and says he was never nervous pitching. Not once. He told me that the only time he was nervous in sports was when he played golf with Bobby Orr.

I mentioned Rickey Henderson recently, and can't let him go with just one cursory reference. This guy was a classic. He truly is a Hall of Fame player, but an occasional lack of hustle was maddening to managers. In fact, such an incident ended his Mets career. One night at Shea, he hit a fly ball to left field which he thought was going to be a home run, so he stood at home plate admiring his work. One problem...the ball hit the wall, stayed in play, and the embarrassed Henderson managed only a single. Within days he was released, but when he left he took a lot of levity with him.

He could mangle the English language like few others. When he meant to use the phrase, "let bygones be bygones," what came out was,

"Let bye-byes be bye-byes." He was famous for not knowing teammates' names, but he knew numbers.

For a couple of years in the late 1990s, more than a few players took to stenciling uniform numbers onto their caps. Usually it was done in tribute to a teammate who had been injured, traded, or released, but it really was starting to get out of hand. Rickey, who wore No. 24 for the Mets and often spoke in the third person, took the field one day with a rather large "24" stenciled on the side of his Mets cap. Matt Loughlin, the reporter on our Mets' telecasts asked Henderson to whom that "24" was a tribute. The response? "That's Rickey's number. It's a tribute to Rickey." I'm not sure if he was the only player ever to pay such an homage to himself, but whether it was coincidence or not, shortly thereafter the whole business of players sporting other players' numbers on their caps thankfully came to an end.

If Rickey Henderson was baseball's leader in fractured language, perhaps no one in the history of television sitcoms was more prolific at it than the legendary *All in the Family* patriarch Archie Bunker, played by the late Carroll O'Connor. I loved Archie, and I loved that show. So you can imagine my excitement when I saw Rob Reiner, who played Archie's son-in-law Mike Stivic, the "Meathead," standing in the press box at Dodger Stadium, talking to Dodgers broadcaster Charlie Steiner.

I immediately went to our broadcast booth where I said to "the Immortal" Chris Majkowski, (our producer/engineer and another big fan of the program) that I would give him $50 right then and there if he would go over to Reiner and call him "Meathead." I figured this would be a slam dunk for an enterprising sort like Maj, and it would have been $50 well spent, but somehow he failed to get it done; proving yet again that if you want something accomplished badly enough, you just have to do it yourself.

This was prior to a day game after a night game, and the lineups were slow to be posted. I knew I could sucker Charlie into an introduction, so as I walked toward the two of them, I said "Hey Charlie, it's getting late. Do you guys have a lineup yet?" It worked like a charm.

Charlie said, "Not yet, but say hello to Rob Reiner."

In the ensuing millisecond I told myself that you only go around once, and that in a few years some nice publisher will ask me to write a book and this would make a great story, and so in my best Archie Bunker imitation (and I will admit I do a pretty good one), I said "Aww, hey dere Meathead."

For a second, Reiner looked at me as though he had just bitten into a lemon, and Charlie's jaw dropped as the color drained from his face. I was afraid Reiner was going to hit me and that Steiner was about to have the big one, but before any of that could happen I quickly apologized to Rob, telling him I had been a huge fan of the show, and that I admired the wonderful work he's done since, and I was just looking for a cheap laugh. Thankfully, he "got it" (at least he said he did), and we actually had a very pleasant conversation about baseball. He was a mensch. So was, and is, Charlie, who recovered without the help of paramedics and remains a good friend to this day.

This is no great revelation, but former Dodgers manager Tommy Lasorda is quite the character. Somehow, most Lasorda stories revolve around food, and this one is no different. In fact, the last time I saw him, just a year ago, he came into our Mets radio booth to promote prostate cancer awareness; something he has done for Major League Baseball for more than a decade. I asked him if he could get me a piece of that blueberry pie he just had. When he wondered how I had known that, I pointed to his shirt, which had ingested as much of it as Tommy had. It was a different meal that he enjoyed, though, more than 30 years earlier, which I feared might have gotten me fired.

This is when I was the sports director of WHN Radio in the late 1970s. Being sports director of a country music station is kind of like being captain of a rowboat. I was the only one in the sports department, but it looked great on a business card so I fully embraced the title. Generally, my job consisted of doing morning sports reports and covering games at night, but at this particular time the station wanted me to arrange for sports figures to come to the studio one morning and serve as guest disc jockeys. The station manager, Nick Verbitsky, was a big sports fan, and when I told him I would try to get Joe Torre, who was managing the Mets at the time, Verbitsky saw that the Dodgers were coming to town and asked me to see if Lasorda would be interested in joining Torre.

The toughest part of this assignment was convincing people to come to the studio at 7:00 AM, for no compensation, but somehow I was able to pull it off. Hockey players Dave Maloney and Bryan Trottier, basketball player Bernard King, Giants punter Dave Jennings, and Jets coach Walt Michaels, as well as former Yankee Ron Blomberg all were kind enough to participate and this became quite a feather in my young cap. Lasorda figured to be a challenge, since I didn't know him personally, but the Dodgers' public relations director proved quite helpful, and told me that Lasorda would do it if the station allowed him to take his coaches to dinner on the station's dime. I pleaded with Nick to go along with it, especially since it was his idea, figuring that dinner for five or six couldn't cost as much as the value of the publicity.

Lasorda asked to go to a place called Ponte's, with which Torre had a promotional relationship. I figured that with Joe's connection to the restaurant, the station might get consideration on the bill, so Verbitsky somewhat nervously gave his consent, and one morning in 1979, Joe Torre and Tommy Lasorda were guest DJs on Del DeMontreux's morning show.

The show was a huge hit. Joe and Tommy seemed to enjoy themselves, and everyone at the station appeared to love it; just not as much as Lasorda and his staff enjoyed dinner. When the bill came, I almost went. Nick was rather irate when he was told that Lasorda had signed off on an $800 check. Remember, now, this was 1979, and in today's dollars that would probably amount to somewhere around $2,500. I don't know why, but I think Nick figured it wouldn't cost more than a couple hundred bucks. That might have covered the food, but the bottles of wine sent the total into the stratosphere, and the only thing that kept me from being launched that far was the fact that this was Verbitsky's brainchild and I was just following orders. That was my argument to ensure that I didn't take a financial hit.

All these years later I get a kick out of looking back at those early years of my career, and how everything was new and exciting. Happily, I can report that the here and now remains exciting as well; in fact some of my biggest thrills have come from "looking back."

Many times I have been honored to serve as on-field master of ceremonies for the Mets on days or nights when they've honored championship clubs or former players. One of my favorite such events was the night in 2006 at Shea Stadium when the Mets commemorated the 20th anniversary of the 1986 World Series champions.

The podium was erected at second base, although because it was raining, the tarp was on the field, but the ceremonies took place as scheduled. The location of the podium held particular significance for me. If I have anything resembling a hobby, it's The Beatles, and finding rare recordings or studio outtakes of theirs. Simply put, I have worshipped The Beatles since they arrived in our consciousness in 1964, and as cliché as it sounds, their music truly has served as the soundtrack of my life.

In fact, in the fall of 1980, I was out to dinner with a date who was inquiring about my career. She asked me which player I had most enjoyed meeting or getting to know. I told her that if you put every player I ever met, every player I would meet in the future, and every player I would ever want to meet and put them all in one room, and just put John Lennon in the room next door, without hesitation I would knock on Lennon's door. Within weeks, John Lennon was gone. Given the same hypothetical choice today, I would make the same decision.

This is where that podium comes in. When The Beatles performed their concerts at Shea Stadium in 1965 and 1966, the stage was set up at second base, a fact that I kept reminding myself of as I introduced the 1986 Mets. All through the ceremonies, I flashed back to those concerts and instead of thinking that this is where so many of my favorite players performed over the years, I instead imagined myself in that same spot during those legendary concerts. I could not get out of my head the fact that I was enjoying the exact same view from the exact same vantage point that John, Paul, George, and Ringo had. It was all I could do to avoid breaking into a chorus of "I'm Down" or "Baby's in Black" (which, trust me, wouldn't have done anyone any good). It was an exhilarating, surrealistic experience.

On subsequent occasions, I have been proud to MC the 40th anniversary reunion of the 1969 world champion Mets, the induction of several players into the Mets Hall of Fame, Opening Days, and many other events on either Shea or Citi Field's center stage. It is a huge honor to serve in that role, and no matter how many times I do it, I am always deeply flattered to be asked.

Chapter 19
MELTING POT

I talked earlier about factions in a big-league clubhouse, about baseball being a melting pot that throws together diverse personalities from varying cultures and expects them to live together in harmony. It's almost impossible. Familiarity often breeds contempt. Even families have their disagreements, their feuds.

That brings me to Billy Wagner. Billy is a very intelligent, very aware individual. I love Billy, as a guy and as a pitcher, but by his own admission, he can be a hot-head whose fatal flaw is that, to use the vernacular, he always tells it like it is.

Wagner came to the Mets as a free agent in 2006 after spending nine seasons in Houston and two in Philadelphia as one of the top closers in the game. He's a little guy, only 5'10" and 180 pounds, but he was a fierce competitor and he threw with such torque that he could get it up there at 100 miles an hour. When the Mets got him, he was 34 years old and he had saved 284 games, so he was hardly young, naïve, or immature. Quite the contrary.

As an example of Wagner as a thinking man's pitcher, one day not long after he joined the Mets, I noticed him sitting in the dugout watching the opposing team's batting practice. I went to him and said, "Are you just killing time?"

"Oh, no," he said. "I watch the other team hit every day, because I can see who's working on something and what that something is. If a hitter is working on going the other way, or if a guy is working on handling the inside pitch, they're showing me what their vulnerabilities are and I can use that."

I had never heard a pitcher say that before.

Wagner is a fierce competitor. He began to notice that if the team lost a game on getaway day, some of the Latin players would appear unperturbed on the plane. By their behavior, you couldn't tell if the team won or lost and that devil-may-care attitude rankled his old-school approach to the game. To be happy or playful after a loss was completely contrary to Wagner's nature and abhorrent to him, but being the thinking man he is, he went to Luis Castillo, a veteran from San Pedro de Macoris in the Dominican Republic, in search of an explanation for such behavior.

"Why is it that half of our guys are sitting here, angry because we lost a game, and some guys have the boom box going and are whooping it up?" Wagner asked. "I don't get it. What's the story?"

"How many games do we play in a year? 162?" Castillo said. "This one's over. There's nothing we can do about it. If I'm sitting around moping, that's not going to change the final score. We have another game to play tomorrow. I'm going to go out tonight and enjoy myself and that's it. That's just the way we are."

Castillo's explanation helped Wagner better understand the thinking of some of his Latin teammates. Still, there was no way he was ever going to be able to relate to that attitude. To his credit, however, Wagner started thinking about this reaction to losing a game and he came to realize that some, if not most of these men, grew up in abject poverty. When they were kids, winning meant having food on the table. Now, they were in the big leagues and they had security and comfort, so they had already won. He could see though, that the game wasn't incidental to them for the three hours they were between the lines. They played hard. They wanted to win as badly as anyone. They hated losing. But when the game was over, it was over, and it was too late to worry about it. It was time to move on to the next game.

"I can't relate to it," Wagner said. "I don't agree with it, but I have a better understanding of it after talking to some of the guys."

I don't know if Wagner ever fully came to grips with the situation, but I have enormous respect for him because he took the trouble to seek answers to the questions that were bothering him.

Two players who have always had the respect of their teammates are Pedro Martinez and Johan Santana—prideful competitors who are serious and intelligent students of their craft.

There are two things I experienced with Martinez that caught my interest, one has to do with baseball and the other has nothing whatsoever to do with baseball. The baseball story occurred in '05, his first year with the Mets. Early in the season, Pedro was pitching against the Astros in Shea Stadium. It's well known in baseball circles that many pitchers are so anal in their preparation that if anything changes at all they become discombobulated to the point that it could affect their performance. This day, Martinez was taking his warm-up tosses between innings and somehow the sprinklers accidentally went off, shooting water all around the infield. If that happened to some pitchers, they might not have been able to pitch the game. But Pedro stood on the mound, enjoying the water dripping on him, laughing and dancing around. He had a ball with it. That's exactly the sort of thing that rubs off positively on a team. There never was anything uptight about Pedro. Everything was loosey-goosey, until the game began, and then he was all business, as serious and competitive as anyone I have ever seen.

The other incident occurred at an airport. I was standing near Martinez on the tarmac waiting to board a team charter. I wasn't eavesdropping, but I was close enough to him that I could overhear him talking on the telephone. I have no idea who he was talking to or what the context was; it doesn't matter. This is what I heard:

"Do you suffer from amnesia?"

Who speaks like that? Not even someone who grew up in the United States would express himself that way, but here was this man who talked

And here I am making like a real big-league pitcher at Mets Fantasy Camp in 1988. Obviously, I did not master the drop-and-drive delivery.

often about sitting under a mango tree when he was a kid growing up in the Dominican Republic, and he's on the phone and instead of saying something like, "What, you don't remember?" he says "Do you suffer from amnesia?"

So many players that grow up outside of the United States and adopt English as their second language learn just enough to put a few thoughts together. Not Pedro. He was going to embrace the English language as his own and articulate it as well as he could. I couldn't be more impressed. To me it was a window into his intellect, which was evident not only in how he conducted himself on the pitcher's mound but also in the way he spoke.

Johan Santana rivals Martinez's competitiveness, his pitching intelligence, and his professionalism, he just doesn't quite have Pedro's lightheartedness, and his outgoing, fun-loving personality. Johan is all business, at least in comparison to Pedro.

The game I will always remember about Santana was on a Saturday afternoon in '08, Johan's first season as a Met. The Mets were trying to stave off a collapse for the second straight season. The year before, they blew a seven-game lead in the final 2½ weeks and failed to make the playoffs. Now they had held a 3½ game lead in the National League East on September 10, and 17 days later, on the next-to-last day of the season, they were two games behind the Phillies in the NL East and a game behind Milwaukee for the wild-card with two games to play.

Nobody knew that Santana had a torn meniscus, and yet on only three days' rest he pitched a complete-game, three-hit, nine-strikeout shutout in a 2–0 victory over the Florida Marlins.

That was Johan displaying the heart of a lion. I could see what made him so special in the American League all those years. The Mets had lost to the Marlins on Friday night and they had the memory of the year before weighing them down. If ever a team needed to be picked up by the neck and resuscitated it was that team, and Johan did that in a way that was just remarkable, especially when we later found out that he had the torn meniscus.

The sad thing about Santana is that in his first three seasons with the Mets, he had three major surgeries, one after each year: knee, elbow, and shoulder. Of course, his signature performance with the Mets would turn out to be his no-hitter against the Cardinals on June 1, 2012. After tormented Mets manager Terry Collins, against his better judgment, had allowed Santana to complete his gem by throwing a career-high 134 pitches with a surgically repaired shoulder, his first words to Santana were, "You're my hero." Poignant stuff.

In some ways, Jose Reyes is the anti–Pedro Martinez/Johan Santana. It's not that Reyes isn't a competitor and that he doesn't care about winning; he is and he does. But he's one of those fun-loving guys who believe that when the game is over, it's over. If you lose, you go about your business and prepare for the next game. Often, that attitude is misinterpreted as a lack of caring.

Jose has a way of being petulant on the field. If things don't go his way, he'll turn his back on the first baseman when they're throwing the ball around the infield between innings. There was also a time when Reyes was upset about something and he threw his glove down on the ground like a Little Leaguer. It looked awful and unprofessional, and Keith Hernandez, who was as competitive as they come when he was a player and now is outspoken as a broadcaster, took Jose to task on the air about his lack of maturity.

Reyes heard about Keith's comments and on a Mets charter he walked up to Hernandez and said, almost in a threatening way, "You never made an error?"

Jose was angry and confrontational when Pedro Martinez came from several rows back and, instead of going to Reyes, as you might expect, he went to Keith, who he knows and respects, put his arm around him, and said, "Don't worry about it. I'll take care of it." Pedro then gently admonished Reyes by saying, "Let's go. Get back." With that, Pedro, in his innate wisdom, was able to curtail what could have been a serious incident and an ugly scene.

I enjoyed being around Reyes when he was with the Mets. You always felt good when you were around him because there were a lot of laughs. Except for those rare moments of petulance, Jose is a fun guy, always upbeat and always with that infectious smile. He surprised me one day during the winter by showing up at a New York Islanders game I was broadcasting. Jose was living on Long Island and he had never been to a hockey game (I don't think they play much hockey in the Dominican Republic), so he came to Nassau Coliseum and even came up to the broadcast booth to say hello, which I thought was very nice of him.

Chapter 20
ALL THE WRIGHT STUFF

want to be extra careful here because I don't want to embarrass him, nor do I want to suggest he is perfect, completely devoid of human frailties, totally incapable of any negative thought, word, or deed.

That being said, now hear this:

David Wright is the guy you'd want your daughter to marry.

I say that as the father of two grown daughters, not that this is a proposal of any kind. It's simply the admiration and respect I have for Wright as a young man, which does not come casually or from a small sampling. It's the culmination of firsthand, up-close observation on an almost daily basis for a period of six to eight months a year over a span of nearly a decade, in a variety of situations, dealing with people from various walks of life.

In all that time, in every situation, on good days or bad, under the most intense scrutiny, during success and failure, in good health or injured, I have never once seen him deviate from his good-guy persona, have never heard anybody say a bad word about him. Never!

If Tom Seaver was "the Franchise" for the Mets, David Wright is the current "Face of the Franchise"—its best player, its spokesperson, its go-to guy with the media, a leader, a role model, a tireless worker, a player with an impeccable image—and he has been almost from the first day he showed up on July 21, 2004.

Like most people, I am a creature of habit. I have my idiosyncrasies, especially when it comes to how I spend my day in preparation for broadcasting a game when I'm on the road. I love having lunch by myself because those are the couple of hours of the day that belong to me. Everything else when you're working revolves around being part of a group, but the few hours when I can work out in the morning, then go to a restaurant for a casual lunch, be by myself, read the newspapers, unwind, and get ready at the same time, those hours to me are golden.

On more than one occasion, I'd be in a restaurant having lunch, and then I'd ask for the check and be told, "It's already been taken care of."

"What?"

The waiter or waitress will point to the corner and there's David Wright. Many among the Mets' contingent share that story.

Every once in a while, when the opportunity presented itself, I've returned the favor when I'd see him in a restaurant and be able to pick up his check. Invariably, at the ballpark that night, David will come up to me and say, "Now what are you doing that for?"

And my reaction is, "Yeah, exactly. Right back at you."

That's the kind of man he is. He's as special a person as he's perceived to be by those who portray him as being just that way.

When a guy comes with a certain reputation—and I did this with Gary Carter—I have a tendency to look very hard to find the crack in that reputation. It wasn't there with Carter and it's not there with David Wright. Not that I've seen. There's always the chance that when someone seems too good to be true, that he's going to be two-faced in some way; that somebody is going to say, "I know you all think he's the greatest guy in the world, but he's not exactly all that he's cracked up to be."

Nobody has ever said that to me about David. I've talked to a lot of baseball people privately: players, front-office people, writers, and I have never heard anybody say a bad word about David Wright.

With fans, he's absolutely ridiculous in how he deals with them. An example! In spring 2012, from about 50 to 100 feet away he spotted a young kid wearing a David Wright jersey. Without being asked, David grabbed a baseball, walked over to the kid, asked the kid if he had a pen, took the pen, signed the baseball, and gave it to the kid. I've seen him do similar things dozens of times.

I can't emphasize how much I abhor certain social media, like Twitter and blogs. In this environment where everybody is a "journalist" and everybody has his own "newspaper" or his own "column" and writes his own headlines, even a minor celebrity is under constant scrutiny and gets put in a position where he can be made to look like something he's not. The fact that it hasn't happened to David is even further substantiation of his character.

It's obvious that his parents did a wonderful job in raising David. His father is in law enforcement in Virginia, and discipline was ingrained in

Here I am with David Wright and Ike Davis. (Photo: Marc S. Levine, New York Mets)

David from his earliest days, and it shows. He's totally real. Everything about him is genuine.

As the face of the franchise and the Mets' oldest player in terms of service, David Wright sets the tone in the clubhouse, just as Mike Piazza did before him, Keith Hernandez did before Piazza, and Tom Seaver did before Hernandez. As a role model, Wright has had a positive effect on those who arrived after him. Happily, David is now in position to become the Mets' first "franchise player" to play with the team for the entirety of his career after signing an eight-year contract following the 2012 season. That honor could not be bestowed on a more worthy person.

Although he's eight years older than Wright and made his major league debut when David was still in high school, R.A. (for Robert Allen) Dickey is a relative newcomer to the Mets and not the type you would expect to be a team leader. For one thing, it's difficult for a starting pitcher, who works every five days, to assume that role, unless he happens to have the status of a Tom Seaver.

Dickey is someone who, instead of wearing a baseball uniform on the mound, would be just as comfortable wearing a herringbone jacket with elbow patches and a pipe coming out of his mouth. That's exactly who he is. R.A. will be a college professor some day, because that's one of his passions. You never get the stock answers from him, there's always a lot of thought behind what he says.

There was a game in Chicago in '11, a cold, slick, raw day. Dickey was pitching and Daniel Murphy was playing first base. A ball was hit to the right side and Dickey was late getting off the mound because he thought Murphy was going to make the play, which he should have. But Murph was playing in place of an injured Ike Davis, and he hesitated, so R.A. had to bust it to first base and in so doing he hurt his Achilles, albeit not seriously, but it set him back about a week.

Some days later, I was talking with Dickey and I asked him about the play. The easiest thing for Dickey would have been to bury Murphy, who had left his pitcher out to dry and had actually blamed himself for the injury. If he chose to, Dickey could have told me privately that Murphy was at fault because I didn't have a microphone and it was obvious I wasn't interviewing him for attribution. This type of scenario is where players often criticize teammates.

Instead, Dickey showed how kind he was by his answer to my question. He was very humble about it. "I understand Murph might have made the play himself," he said, "but I don't want to blame him. It was on me."

That's Dickey. He's very introspective, considerate, and compassionate, exactly what you expect from him based on how he has been portrayed. His 2012 Cy Young Award–winning season was one of the most memorable single-season performances by a Mets player in the history of the franchise. However, with the Mets looking to expedite their path to contention, general manager Sandy Alderson traded Dickey to the Toronto Blue Jays for two blue-chip prospects: catcher Travis d'Armaud and pitcher Noah Syndergaard. If either or both youngsters pan out, R.A. Dickey might not yet be finished helping the New York Mets.

Daniel Murphy to me is someone with a typical baseball background. The star of his Little League team, his high school team, his college team, a prospect that rose up the ladder in the Mets farm system, from rookie league to Class A to Class AA to Class AAA to the big leagues. You get the feeling he's very comfortable and appreciates being a big leaguer.

There are times I want so hard for Murphy to succeed because he wants it so badly. He's a guy who doesn't play any position instinctively, mainly because he's always been bounced from one position to another. His best position is with a bat, so he may eventually wind up in the American League as a designated hitter. He is a legitimate hitter, although his hard work has made him a serviceable second baseman.

I feel for him because I know how much it killed him to miss so much time with serious injuries in '10 and '11. When you see a young guy being helped off the field near tears as much for his own career prospects as for the pain that he's feeling, you can't help but root for a guy like that. It's been a struggle at times for Murphy to firmly establish himself in the big leagues, but he's a good kid who is worth rooting for.

On the other hand, Ike Davis is going to be a star in the Big Apple if he performs, because he gets it. He's mature beyond his years. He's New York savvy even though he didn't grow up in New York (he was born in Minnesota and raised in Arizona). People say he's got baseball bloodlines (his dad, Ron, pitched for 11 seasons with the Twins, Yankees, Cubs, Giants, and Dodgers), but he never saw his dad pitch. Ike was a year old when Ron retired from baseball.

Davis struggled terribly in the first two months of the 2012 season, but rebounded to hit 32 homers and drive in 90 runs. His name surfaced in trade rumors in 2012, but if he does stick around, the ultra-confidant Ike should be a fan favorite for years.

As a rookie in 2010, Lucas Duda was a very shy and quiet kid. You don't need a psychiatrist's license to know that his shyness came from a lack of confidence in his ability to play in the big leagues. He even spoke openly about that lack of confidence, which made Terry Collins unhappy because he thought that was a window into his persona that pitchers could exploit.

The next year, Duda had some success. He showed he has tremendous power, hitting 10 home runs and batting .292, and the change in him was miraculous. During spring training '12, I had a 10-minute conversation with him (I could never have had that long a discussion with him in his first two years) and found him to be a nice, easygoing guy. That bodes well for him because now he feels that he belongs. He struggled in 2012, but the Mets need his power.

For someone so young, Josh Thole, who was drafted and signed right out of high school, has been saddled with a heavy burden, charged with handling the Mets' pitching staff in addition to serving as the team's player representative. He's a nice kid and it goes without saying that he's obviously bright and has the respect of his teammates.

If the Mets are going to charge back to being the perennial contenders that they once were, these are some of the guys who are going to help them get there.

EPILOGUE

The 2011 season marked my 25th year with the New York Mets, a quarter-of-a-century connection with my boyhood team, a good time to pause for reflection.

In those 25 years, the Mets won 2,017 games and lost 1,962, a mere 55 games over .500 in a quarter of a century. They had 13 winning seasons and 12 losing ones. They finished last in their division three times and made the playoffs four times, reaching the World Series only once, in 2000, when they were knocked off by their crosstown rivals, the Yankees.

In '11, the Mets finished in fourth place in the five-team National League East with a record of 77–85. It was their third consecutive losing season and, from all reports and by the reckoning of most "experts," the end of the decline was nowhere in sight. As the '12 season beckoned, many of my friends, well-meaning, sympathetic, solicitous, and compassionate, said to me, "You must dread this upcoming season."

My reaction?

Dread this season? Are you nuts? I would only dread it if I had to have a job. I have an avocation. I have a lifelong love for the Mets, for broadcasting and for baseball, for being at the ballpark. However this season evolves I'm going to relish the chance to watch kids like Lucas Duda, Ike Davis, Ruben Tejada, and the pitchers on their way up, Zack

Wheeler and Matt Harvey, grow into bona fide major leaguers. When the day comes, and hopefully it's this year, but if it's not, whenever it is that the Mets become winners again I will feel enriched by having had the experience of watching those kids develop into championship level players.

As the season goes on and if the team is once again in the doldrums, then each game becomes a separate entity. If you look at being out of contention as a three-month endeavor, it's logical to ask how am I going to do 80 games for three months when the games mean virtually nothing? It can be a daunting prospect.

It may sound idiotic when players and managers say they take the games one at a time, but the truth of the matter is that's exactly how I look upon what I am asked to do every day, every season, 162 times. Every broadcast, representing every game, is a totally different entity. I might decide on my way to the ballpark—and I've done this—that there is something mechanical that I want to work on, kind of like a pitcher experimenting with a new pitch in game conditions. I might want to work on calling a particular play a little bit differently, or I might want to incorporate something in my routine that I haven't used before and that challenge will get me through that game or a string of games while I search to refine whatever it is I'm looking to improve upon.

Even though the buildup to the game might become somewhat laborious and is something you might not have as much energy for as you did when they were winning, the minute the umpire gives the ball to the pitcher and points to him and says, "Play ball!" everything starts again. It's fresh. There is the possibility that this will be the day a Mets pitcher throws a(nother) no-hitter, or this may be the day somebody does something I've never seen before on a baseball field. And because I love the mechanics of what I do—I still love calling a baseball game—when that pitcher throws the first pitch, I'm doing what I love doing. Sure, it's easier when you're covering a winning team, when you're in the midst of the excitement of a pennant race, but I also embrace the challenge of trying to keep my listeners interested and focused and entertained.

When people tell me, "You must be dreading this season" (whatever that season is), what goes through my mind is that in 1968, the Mets won 73 games—that's fewer than the Mets won in '11 and '12—and a year later they won the World Series. So if it could happen in '69 when it was so unexpected, why can't it happen in '13 or '14 or '15? Hope springs eternal. Every spring.

Obviously, the '13 Mets won't have Seaver, Koosman, Gentry, and Ryan lined up to get them home, but back in '69 we didn't know

Emceeing Opening Day ceremonies at Citi Field as the Mets begin their 50th anniversary season on April 5, 2012. (Photo: Marc S. Levine, New York Mets)

that Seaver, Koosman, Gentry, and Ryan were going to be SEAVER, KOOSMAN, GENTRY, and RYAN. Who knows? Zack Wheeler and Matt Harvey could be this generation's Seaver and Koosman.

So I'm no less enthusiastic about a season starting now than I was in '69, but the reward then was unexpected and everlasting, and there's a 15-year-old kid out there who hopefully will one day experience the same euphoria I did when his team exceeds all expectations and shocks the baseball world by winning the World Series against overwhelming odds. That 15-year-old is going to be able to look back at those years he spent watching that crop of kids develop into big leaguers that he would embrace and treasure. It's a continuum. You're not in a vacuum. It's not just this season.

Looking back, as a kid the 1970 baseball season was torture for me. Maybe it was because years before I had grown used to seeing the Yankees win year after year after year, but somehow I felt that if the Mets didn't win again in '70 it would invalidate what happened in '69; that if they were no longer world champions, it's almost as if their championship season never happened. The Mets didn't win in '70, they finished third, six games behind the Pirates and Cubs, but what you learn as you get older is that even though they didn't win in '70, the Mets were the '69 champions of baseball forever.

When I started working for the Mets in 1987, the year after they won the World Series, and was doing a talk show, I approached it with that theme. Billy Joel had a song, "This Is the Time (to Remember)" and I used it occasionally in and out of commercials because I wanted people to understand that it was a great time to be a Mets fan. They were world champions, they had a great team. My message was, "They may win this year and they may not, but if they don't it doesn't mean that they didn't win in '86."

That thought was hammered home to me watching the football Giants celebrate their 2012 Super Bowl championship with a parade down Broadway in New York City. I wanted to shout out to the people there to embrace every minute of what they were experiencing, because they're going to look back 30 years from now at how great it was to have had anything to do with being a Giants fan. Just soak it all in.

The Giants victory in '12 was a particularly good illustration, because after 14 games they were 7–7, and who could have predicted they would finish as they did? Raise your hand if you saw it coming!

So, yes, miracles do happen in sports, and despair is a wasted emotion. Embrace the good times and understand that if you don't suffer through the difficult times, you can't properly appreciate the great times.

Dread this or any other season?

I think often of something my friend and former broadcast partner Ralph Kiner once said. The Mets had finished a particularly bad season and as we were wrapping up the final game, on the air I said to Ralph, "It's been quite a season. What are your thoughts about the end of it, and are you happy it's over?"

And Kiner, in his infinite wisdom and with the experience of more than 70 baseball seasons—not all of them championship ones—said, "You're always glad when the season ends, but a month later you can't wait for the next one to get started."

My sentiments exactly!

Acknowledgments

I've never written a book before so the temptation in listing acknowledgments is to mention everyone I have ever come in touch with so nobody's feelings are hurt. I'm told by the publisher that such behavior will terminate our agreement and prevent the book from ever being published, so if your name is not listed here my intent was to include you, but business is business.

I will start by thanking Triumph Books and Jesse Jordan for approaching me with this project and most importantly for pairing me with Phil Pepe. Phil has been a giant in the New York newspaper business since as far back as I can remember. (Sorry, Phil. They have fact checkers and I started reading the papers when I was very, very young.) I thoroughly enjoyed the time we spent together working on this, and one of these days I would like to do a show with him to look back on his fabulous career. I'm sure Phil will join me in thanking the nice people at the Bayside Diner who allowed us to sit there for hours on end as we put the pieces of this work together.

I have been blessed to work for and with people who have enabled me to broadcast games in my hometown for the entirety of my career. Thank you to Fred Wilpon, Saul Katz, and Jeff Wilpon, owners of the New York Mets, and to the very special people in their front office, Dave Howard,

Dave Newman, Sandy Alderson, John Ricco, Lorraine Hamilton, Jay Horwitz, Shannon Forde, Ethan Wilson, and all of the fine people who make a ballclub tick. Your continued help and support mean the world to me. Special thanks to the Mets' fabulous team photographer, Marc Levine.

From the early days of my career at WHN, I will always be thankful to Charlie Kaye, Ed Salamon, Nick Verbitsky, Gene Ladd, Larry Kenney, Del DeMontreaux, and Dan Taylor, those I worked either for or with and who all were valued friends and/or associates.

No one has been more influential in my career than Marv Albert. I started his fan club in 1967, and all these years later I still consider myself the president of the Marv Albert Fan Club. There are no term limits, so I hold that title in perpetuity. I humbly thank Marv as well for his wonderful and flattering foreword to this book.

WFAN has felt like home since Day 1 in 1987. Mark Mason, Eric Spitz, and Mark Chernoff have been instrumental in making that station tick and my job truly an avocation.

I have had some wonderful broadcast partners over the years. Sal "Red Light" Messina is a hockey Hall of Famer for good reason. He put up with me for six full years and parts of others with the Rangers. Joe Micheletti, a former Islanders partner, is simply one of the finest human beings in the world. The eight years I worked with him were a gift.

I have also been blessed to work with Gary Cohen, truly a kindred spirit, Ron Darling, Keith Hernandez, Ralph Kiner, Fran Healy, Ed Westfall, Billy Jaffe, Butch Goring, Tom McCarthy, Wayne Hagin, Ed Coleman, Josh Lewin, and Jim Duquette as on-air partners. I am not sure what I value more, your partnership or your friendship, and that goes for all of my broadcast cohorts. Included in that list should be "the immortal" Chris Majkowski, the best radio producer-engineer in the business. Dov Kramer and John Schweibacher are valuable associates on the WFAN Mets Radio Network.

People I have worked with in hockey, Barry Watkins, Chris Botta, Kimber Auerbach, Sam Rosen, John Davidson, and many others have made my job fun and easy. I especially thank Charles Wang, owner of the New York Islanders, for his support over many years, and the same goes for Mike Milbury, longtime Islanders general manager, as well as Islanders executives Michael Picker and Paul Lancey.

Many executives at Madison Square Garden Network have been supportive and instrumental, from Phil Harmon and Pete Silverman to Joe Cohen, Mike McCarthy, and Leon Schweier to Dan Ronayne, Jeff Filippi, Kevin Meininger, and Leslie Howlett. Additionally I have worked with some terrific behind-the-scenes TV folks such as Larry Roth, Charlie Cucchiara, Matt Borzello, Bill Webb, John Moore, Jim Daddona, Paula McHale, Eric Hornick, JT Townsend, and John Ackerina. Friends and colleagues all. Thanks as well to my longtime agent, Craig Fenech. And a special thanks to Dr. Robert Joseph for the thorough once-over and always sound advice.

I'm getting to the point where I am going to be guilty of leaving people out that I really intend to acknowledge, but please know that in some way, large or small, you have had a role in advancing my career and making this book possible.

And for my many grade school teachers who suggested that I stop reading sports books and move on to something else, okay, I took your advice. I wrote one instead.

ABOUT THE AUTHORS

Howie Rose grew up in Bayside, Queens, as a Mets fan and has been one of the team's broadcasters on radio or television since 1987. Rose was also a talk show host on WFAN for eight years, as well as calling games for the New York Rangers and New York Islanders on radio and television.

Phil Pepe has covered sports in New York for more than five decades. He was the Yankees beat writer for the *New York World Telegram & Sun* from 1961 to 1964 and for the *New York Daily News* from 1971 to 1984. He has written almost 50 books.